FROM THE WORLD OF MUSIC

VOLUME ONE

Essays from the World of Music

ERNEST NEWMAN

Essays from 'The Sunday Times'

Selected by

FELIX APRAHAMIAN

JOHN CALDER

LONDON

First published in Great Britain 1956 by John Calder (Publishers) Ltd.,
18 Brewer Street London W1R 4AS
Re-issued in 1976.
© John Calder (Publishers) Ltd., 1956, 1976

ISBN 0 7145 3548 6 Casebound
ISBN 0 7145 3587 7 Paper

These articles are published with the permission of *The Sunday Times* and
are printed from writings by Ernest Newman during the last fifty-six years.

Front panel and frontispiece photographs by Felix Aprahamian

Printed and bound by Billing & Sons Limited
London, Guildford and Worcester.

CONTENTS

CONTENTS *(continued)*

FOREWORD

THOMAS CARLYLE, in a preface to a reprint that
had been called for of an earlier work of his of which,
apparently, he had come to think less highly than he
had done at one time, lamented that it is not possible
for an author to dispose of his earlier books for good
and all by the simple process by which one gets rid
of one's old horses—by shooting them through the
head. A journalist may sometimes be permitted to
entertain the same regret with regard to his old
articles. What is he to do, however, if someone else
tries to persuade him that some of these may bear
reprinting years after their original appearance?

Many people whose kindly feeling towards me
has seemed to me to outrun their judgment have
from time to time hinted that they would like to see
a reprint in book form of some of my *Sunday Times*
articles. I have invariably turned down suggestions
of this kind, and that for two reasons. In the first
place I find it difficult to be passionately interested
in my own past. The man who has been constrained
by the Fates to spend many years of his life in
musical journalism is a being to be pitied rather
than censured. He cannot, if he has a particle of
sober sense, flatter himself that he has any future.
If he is remembered by a following generation at all
it will be mostly by his blunders: if Hanslick and
certain others of his kidney had not made the
donkeys they did of themselves by the nonsense they

talked about Wagner would even their names have survived to the present day?

On the other hand, in so far as a critic succeeds in talking some sense about contemporary composers and movements he will not get any credit for it later; for what he had to say will by then be regarded as so self-evident that no particular credit attaches to anyone for having said it.

And—to get back to my personal case—in the second place for no inducement whatever would I have shouldered the job of reading through a host of old articles of mine for the purpose of bringing out a selection from them in book form.

To my surprise, however, I discovered one day that this painful task had been quietly undertaken, unknown by me, by my publisher Mr. John Calder and my colleague, Mr. Felix Aprahamian. How the latter managed to plod through file after file of the *Sunday Times* in a search for articles of mine that might be made into a book is simply beyond my comprehension. However, he and Mr. Calder did manage to get through this tedious task, and one day they presented me with a *fait accompli*.

All I have had to do in connection with the present book is to read the proofs. Not only the choice of articles but the arrangement and the systematised grouping of them are entirely the work of the two accoucheurs of the present volume. I have made no alterations in the text of any of the articles. The reader can hardly fail to observe that several of them treat of essentially the same subjects. This is not the result of any calculation at any time on my part: it has largely arisen simply from the fact that in the course of one's weekly work on a paper much the same problems crop up for discussion again and again in some concert hall or opera house or other, each time, however, under a fresh aspect; I am credibly informed, indeed, that even now I occasionally turn out an article on some such basic theme as conducting, operatic singing, Lieder-singing, opera production, Wagner staging, musical criticism, etc. My excuse is simply that questions of this kind have a regrettable habit of confronting the musical journalist time after time in the ordinary course of his duties.

The date of the original appearance of each article is given. It will be seen that in their totality they cover a space of time of many years; and the volume may therefore have at any rate the virtue of presenting the music lover of today with some sort of a picture of the musical activities of the immediate and fairly distant past.

October, 1956.

Ernest Newman

To

VERA

PART I

CRITICS AND CRITICISM

A 'PHYSIOLOGY' OF CRITICISM

I

16th December 1928

Any attempt to give a scientific basis to musical criticism, or even the suggestion that such a thing may some day be possible, is sure to be greeted by the confraternity with loud jeers. Then is the voice of the amateur and the dilettante once more heard in the land: criticism, we are told, is merely a matter of personal reaction to the work of art, and as no two temperaments are alike, no two reactions can be alike. All the critic has to do is to describe how the work has affected *him*, and leave the reader to agree with him or not, as he chooses.

In a sense this is true; the personal equation does come into play in our judgments of art. But so far from this plain and obvious statement representing the last word in criticism, it really represents hardly the first. The public quite rightly mistrusts 'the critics' because they all say different things about the same work; and I confess that I have great sympathy with the public on this point. If 'criticism' means merely your telling other people the effect the work of art has had on you, I cannot see that they can be expected to be vastly interested in that. And for my own part I long ago gave up reading that kind of criticism. I want a form of criticism that will tell me more about the object criticised and less about the critic. A man writes a couple of columns, for instance, declaring that Beethoven is a dullard. After a glance at the article, having got the gist of it, I decline to read any further. I am quite willing to learn something new about Beethoven; but I have no time to waste in reading how Beethoven affects Tom, Dick or Harry. 'Talk to me about Beethoven,' I say to him, 'and I will read you.' 'I *am* talking about Beethoven,' he replies. And my rejoinder is, 'No, you are not telling me anything about Beethoven; you are only telling me something about yourself— how you feel when you listen to Beethoven—and in that subject, I regret to say, I haven't the leisure to take an absorbing interest.'

13

I shall be met with a *tu quoque*, of course: 'What is *your* criticism, then,' I shall be asked, 'but the expression of a personal reaction?' Quite so: and in so far as it is that and nothing more I should be the last man in the world to expect anyone to agree with me, or to go on reading me if he finds himself in regular disagreement with me. I am perfectly willing that my own criticism shall be included in my contemptuous denunciation of criticism in general,—perfectly willing, like Wagner's Wotan, to 'will my own destruction' with a view to the general betterment. My sole concern is not to justify my own amateurishness as against that of other people, but to find, if possible, a more solid basis for criticism than the personal reaction of the moment.

We might begin with small things; and I venture to suggest that before we indulge as we do in the higher flights of musical psychology we ought to work out some sort of a system of musical physiology. Let the poetic fancy play at will on the musical material offered by a composer's work, and we get a species of writing that is very readable and superficially plausible, but has often the minimum of relation to the facts.

A typical specimen of this kind of writing is the much-praised 'Beethoven' of Paul Bekker, that has been hailed in some quarters as the best of all books on Beethoven, but that, from the strictly musical point of view, I myself would regard as one of the worst—that is to say, one of the least *musical*, from a musician's point of view. Bekker reads things into Beethoven's music that are not to be found in the music, while the procedures in the music upon which he bases his poetic fancies are susceptible of much simpler explanations along purely musical lines. This is a typical case of a critic indulging in the psychology of a musical subject before he has mastered its physiology. But it is a form of indulgence that virtually all critics permit themselves, for it is easier to give the fancy its rein than to sit down to the patient discovery of facts.

Let me make clear to the reader, by a specific instance, what I mean by a physiology of musical criticism. The other evening Casals took the andante con moto of Schubert's C major symphony at such a speed that to many of us it seemed all con moto and no andante; allegro molto would have been the proper marking for such a pace. Who is to say that Casals was wrong, however? If we tell him that our feeling of the music is against such a tempo, he would reply that that is how *he* feels it, and his feeling is as good as ours. If we want to *prove* him wrong, we must have recourse not merely to feelings, but to matters that are capable of proof.

I believe it possible, by careful analysis, to establish in each composer's work a physiology of style that is the basis of his psychology. I have suggested the title 'finger-prints' for the elements in a composer's style that are purely personal to him. In 'The Unconscious Beethoven' I tried to establish one of these finger-prints—an ascending figure of three adjacent notes —but, judging from the reviewers' comments, with small success. Indeed, most reviewers missed the point completely. One or two sagely remarked that they could produce passages from Beethoven in which three *descending* notes occurred. This, truly, was an epoch-making revelation; the dicovery that notes sometimes go down as well as up is one that ought to immortalise the name of the genius who first hit upon it. The point was, however, not that Beethoven was the only composer who ever wrote three ascending notes in conjunct motion—which would be a nonsensical thing to assert—but that he is the only composer in whom you will find such a sequence of three notes used with such frequency, always at the same equivalent point in the melody, and always as the obvious expression of a certain state of mind. The three-note sequence, I contend, is a veritable Beethoven finger-print, because it is not found in any other composer.

I have worked for some years at this subject, in connection with other composers besides Beethoven, and I have come to the conclusion that, stylistically, each of them proceeds unconsciously on a few basic formulae. Beethoven's procedure consists of some half-dozen formulae, and the mystery is how, out of these, he should have been able to evolve so infinite a world of expression. Always when he is in a certain mood or wishes to produce a certain effect he is found unconsciously turning to the melodic and rhythmic formula that, for him, is inseparably associated with that mood or that effect. The formula takes so many outward shapes that we may listen to him all our lives and not suspect the existence of it; but once we become aware of it we find it underlying all the superficial modifications it undergoes in this work or that.

Knowledge of this kind of the elements of a composer's style is not merely interesting from the scientific-analytic point of view. It is not a mere curiosity: it has a practical aesthetic value. For while on the one hand we see a certain mood always realised through a certain formula, on the other hand whenever we meet with the formula we are entitled to infer the mood.

Now suppose we had worked out in this way the constituent elements of Schubert's style—not at all a difficult task. Suppose we had found that, in the bulk of his work, a certain technical procedure was always unconsciously employed when Schubert wished to express a certain mood. If, then, we found the same formula in a work that, through the lack of more precise directions on his part, different conductors look at from different points of view, should we not be justified in saying 'Here is the formula that we know to have been used again and again by Schubert for a particular emotional purpose: is it not a fair inference, then, that when he uses it here his purpose was the same as in the other cases, and therefore the work is to be taken at a certain tempo and in a certain mood, and no other?'

The same problem is raised (and could be solved in the same way) by the repeated hammering notes in the finale of the symphony. To one conductor they mean one thing, to another, another, and to a third, nothing at all. But a scientific analysis of Schubert's style would show quite definitely what they mean. Apart, then, from all questions of 'criticism,' I would urge that on the practical aesthetic side alone a good deal would be achieved if for a few years writers upon music would abandon their too easy psychological methods—which mean, in the last resort, only saying the first thing that comes into your head— and devote themselves to establishing a preliminary physiology of each of the great composers' styles.

II

27th January 1929

FROM letters that have reached me, and from questions put to me *viva voce*, I see that I am still a long way from having made clear what I mean by a physiology of criticism. I have been asked, by A, to explain, if I can, how any amount of chemical analysis of the constitution of a flower could help him to enjoy its beauty and its scent. By B I have been asked whether the play of the critic's mind upon the work of a composer may not give the reader a new insight into the latter.

I would reply, briefly, that these points have the minimum of relation to the one I am discussing. Just as we admire a flower for other than chemical reasons, so we 'like' this or that composer for reasons unconnected with technical analysis. Of the latter, indeed, the plain man is incapable, for lack of the necessary knowledge: his reactions to the music are instinctive, and probably depend for their colour much less on the nature of the music than on his own nature. About these instinctive aesthetic reactions, as I have already said, there is no arguing. A man falls in love with a particular musical work as he falls in love with a particular woman, for reasons he could hardly formulate in a way that would carry conviction to other men. We can only leave him to his own raptures, and ask him to leave us to ours. All I have to say on that subject at present is that I can no more enter into another man's ecstasies over Beethoven or Bach than into his ecstasies over Jane or Gladys; still less am I affected by his lack of enthusiasm over Jane or Gladys if those ladies particularly happen to appeal to me.

As for the play of the critic's mind upon a composer or a work—that is generally supposed to be the beginning and the end of criticism—why, I might perversely ask, should I interest myself in that? I cannot live on *his* enthusiasms, or be content to starve because he rejects food that nourishes *me*. In so far as Robinson's criticism is simply the play of Robinson's temperament upon the music, it will convince Brown only in so far as, in virtue of the similarity between his temperament and Robinson's, he is already of Robinson's opinion, and therefore does not need convincing. It is notorious that we can argue about facts, but not about tastes.

The so-much-admired 'play of the critic's mind' upon the work of art is merely, as far as the reader of the criticism is concerned, the work of art sensed at second or third hand.

It does not come to him in its pure state, but blended with the personality of the critic. The question, then, is whether his tastes lie in the direction of a synthetic product of this kind. Mine, at present, do not: I repeat that I am vastly interested in the composer, but very little interested in the critic. If it is just a mere matter of 'reaction' to the work of art, then I prefer to do my reacting for myself; and I advise everyone to do the same.

Any attempt to evade this dilemma, it seems to me, is bound to end in self-contradiction. I have a pleasing example of this in one of the letters that have reached me this week. 'Arising out of your article,' says my correspondent: 'Can a piece of music have any value at all, apart from one's individual reaction to it; and shouldn't that reaction therefore be of interest to each of us, since it may be the only thing that matters?'

So far he seems to be in agreement with me in my thesis that each of us reacts to the work of art because he is what he is, and that to each of us this is 'the only thing that matters.' But as he goes on, he drifts, it appears to me, into the usual fallacy. He proceeds to argue that the reputation of a composer depends not upon his effect on the individual but upon his effect on the general consciousness. I should reply that so far as that is true, it is a truism that hardly needs formulating; but the truth of it is limited by the fact that there is no such thing as the general consciousness. We may speak of 'Mr Everyman's' reaction to the composer if we like, but only as a figure of speech. The generalisation is invalid. There is no composer, not even the greatest, to whom all musical people react in the same way: in my own circle I know excellent musicians who are almost insensitive to this or that 'master,'—one of them to Palestrina, another to Bach, another to Beethoven, another to Berlioz, and so on. When we speak of a *general* 'reaction,' then, we merely mean the reaction of people who think more or less as we do. We have not solved the problem of the personal equation at all; we have simply collected a number of personal equations of the same kind.

My correspondent continues thus: 'Personally, I think that decision [as to aesthetic values] is greatly influenced by music critics; not that we need take their opinions, but that we weigh the arguments with which they support their opinions. We may then agree with them or not, but we should all profit from seeing a thing, in the light of another's acute mind, and, so far, be influenced.' To this I would reply. Yes, if the 'thing' is something in the domain of facts, for here we are open to reason; but no, if the 'thing' is something in the domain of feeling, in which none of us is open to reason. If A believes that the average rainfall in Blackpool is eleven inches a year, it is open to B to bring him official statistics showing that the average is ten or twelve; and if the figures are convincing, and A is a reasonable man, he will be convinced. But if B says that the climate of Blackpool is the finest in the world, and A knows that he is never well there, or if B says that Blackpool gives people rheumatism, and A has lived there for twenty years without feeling a single twinge, B may talk till he is black in the face without bringing A round to his point of view, because here the twain are dealing not with facts but with individual reactions.

So it is with our aesthetic reactions to music. If, as my correspondent began by saying, a piece of music can have no value at all [to each of us] apart from our individual reaction to it, of what value or interest to us are the reactions of people who are differently constituted? If a man feels as I do about Beethoven, I am not confirmed in my feeling; if he feels differently from me about Beethoven, I am not shaken in my feeling. In either case, being what I am, I can only feel as I do.

But, it may be asked, is it not interesting to see how a work or a composer affects another mind? My answer is, yes, if you are interested in that other mind; but not if you are primarily interested in the work or the composer. For no one can talk about a work without showing it to us not as it is but as it is reflected in his temperament and refracted by it. The spectacle may certainly, in some cases, have an interest of its own; but, in my present hunger to learn something new about the mind of the composer, I confess I am impatient when the critic— quite unconsciously, of course—merely fancies he is revealing the composer when what he is really doing is to reveal himself. I repeat that for my part I can no longer read criticism of this kind. (I may write it, but that is another matter; and I do not expect anyone to read it.) My hunger and thirst are for new light on the *composer's* mind, and on his alone; and I suggest that criticism, instead of attempting, as at present, to make that mind clear to me by mere rhapsody or mere curses—both of which are only the expression of how the mind affects the writer of the criticism—should set to work to beat out some method of understanding composers' minds, and how they work in each individual case.

III

3rd February 1929

To obviate any further misunderstanding, of which there has been enough, in all conscience, already, let me say at once that by a 'physiology' of criticism I do not mean a study of the composer in the light of his nerves and arteries, or even of his liver. Considerations of this kind are indeed essential to our knowledge of the man, and may in some cases throw light on the man's work; but they are alien to the present subject. By a 'physiology' of a composer I mean an analysis of his mind not so much in respect of what it has done but of how it works. My complaint against most musical criticism, as I have already said, is that it tells me far too much about the critic and far too little about the composer. The critic likes or dislikes a work according to whether he can or cannot find *himself* in it; his alleged 'criticism' is merely a naive temperamental or moral reaction to the message of the music.

My contention is that before criticism indulges in these lofty flights it had better begin to learn how to walk. We need a critical apparatus if we are to get any critical results worth having. Temperament will of course have its final say in the matter: the individual will like or dislike a work according to his own make-up. Criticism of this kind will always have a certain interest; but criticism of this kind, I repeat, is more in the nature of a self-confession than of an elucidation of the composer, which is why it mostly either leaves us indifferent or irritates us: for if the critic reacts to the work in the same way as *we* do, his agreement with us adds nothing to our own thrill, and if he reacts in a different way, he and we can only glare defiance at each other, for we cannot understand each other.

Criticism of this sort, no matter how well it may be written, is in the last resort the merest dilettantism. A man need not even be a musician to write it: some of the best writing about music, indeed, of the easy adventures-of-a-soul-among-master-pieces type, has been done by non-musicians; because, while they feel as strongly about the music as the musical critic does, they are often much better hands at writing than he is. What I want is musical criticism by and for musicians; and criticism of that sort must recognise as the object of its study not the critic's own temperament but the composer and the work.

The very diversity of opinion among the critics as to the 'value' of this or that composer's music shows that they have not yet worked out the rudiments of the subject. Since it is so evident that a critic likes or dislikes a composer in virtue of the latter's striking, or failing to strike, on the critic's box, surely the first thing to do is to try to find out why the same composer produces such different effects on different minds. It has apparently never dawned on the critics that there are 'types' of mind as of bodily build. The Germans have made a beginning at the task of distinguishing the various types of artistic mind —Othmar Rutz, for example, in his 'Musik, Wort und Körper als Gemütsausdruck' (1911); but musical criticism in general is still unaware that an inquiry of this sort is necessary before we confidently lay it down that our own view of a particular composer is the right one and that everyone who does not share it is wrong. Each of us has his own way of apprehending the universe, his own method of selecting from the infinite range of experience just what he can organise into shapes of art. But it is not enough to see that the *composer* falls into this 'type' or that; we have to recognise that the *listener* is also of this type or that, and that when type A, let us say, sits in judgment on the music of type B, he is trying it before a tribunal that has no jurisdiction.

The French literary critics are also working at a sort of physiology of criticism when they divide authors into those who are predominantly 'visual' and those who are predominantly 'auditive' in their way of sensing life and expressing it. When a *visuel* passes judgment on an *auditif*, or vice versa, he is not really *judging*, as he imagines himself to be doing; he is merely rejecting a particular way of using words because it does not happen to be his way. The genuine critic stands aside from both *visuels* and *auditifs*. He does not presume to say that either is 'right' or 'wrong': he recognises that each type has its own way of assimilating experience and then expressing it; and his concern is not to 'criticise,' to 'place,' to give school certificates for 'aesthetic value,' but simply to analyse and understand both types. The artists themselves are incapable of this detachment; it is impossible, for example, for a Flaubert to 'like' a Mérimée, for the simple reason that the build of the latter's sentences, his cadences, his rhythms, or the seeming absence of these, are the negation of everything that is most personal in the former. When Flaubert reproached Mérimée for 'the cacophony of some of his concatenations of syllables, the dryness of his phrase-endings, his illogical punctuation,' he was merely revolting against a texture and a rhythm that did not happen to be his own. Proust, on the other hand, greatly as he admired Flaubert, found a certain monotony in his calculated cadences and rhythms. How much of what passes for musical criticism is the mere expression of the critic's personal revolt against a texture, a rhythm, a harmony whose only offence it is that it is the natural expression of a composer who is built on fundamentally other mental lines than the critic's?

Let us take an illustration from music. A little while ago I expressed mild surprise at Ravel's saying that Berlioz could not even harmonise a waltz correctly. From his later remarks to an interviewer it appears that when he said 'waltz' he did not mean 'waltz,' and when he said 'correctly' he did not mean 'correctly,' but that otherwise he adhered to his original statement. (As he has also informed us English that Elgar is not typically English, we have to admit that Ravel's excursions into musical criticism have at any rate the virtue of intrepidity.) He now changes 'correctly' to 'adequately'; and of course *he* is to be the norm by which the adequacy or inadequacy of Berlioz's harmony is to be tested, and therefore, since Berlioz's harmony is, as Ravel admits, 'part of his style, and therefore of himself,' *he* is to be the norm by which the right of Berlioz to be himself, rather than to be Ravel, is to be tested! I regret infinitely that I cannot admit his claim. Is it not clear that what is wrong as between Ravel and Berlioz is very much what is wrong, *mutatis mutandis*, between, say, Mérimée and Flaubert—the pure impossibility of an artist of one type of make-up seeing the matter as an artist of another type sees it?

Ravel's attempts to justify his artistic egoism merely make it worse. He censures Rimsky-Korsakov for finding some of Moussorgsky's harmonies inadequate and rewriting them in his own way; but he will not admit that *he* can be in the wrong in finding Berlioz's harmony inadequate. Because he wants to side with Moussorgsky as against Rimsky-Korsakov he lays down the aesthetic law that 'you cannot alter a composer's harmonies without altering the trend of his music.' To alter Berlioz's harmonies, then, would be to alter the trend of his music. It is no use, therefore, Ravel trying to make out that all that is wrong with Berlioz is that he did not understand harmony: what he really means is that Berlioz had no right to let his music trend in the direction of Berlioz. He ought to have made it trend in the direction of Ravel, just as Flaubert thought that Mérimée would have done better to write not like Mérimée but like Flaubert.

IV

17th February 1929

THE sooner I end this series of articles the better, for it is evident from the letters I receive on the subject that no one has the slightest idea what it is I am driving at. I must wait and see if I have any better luck in a treatment of the subject on a larger scale elsewhere. The term 'physiology' is plainly a stumbling-block for most people; they read into it a meaning I never intended, and then write me long letters that are most interesting in themselves, but hopelessly irrelevant to the theme.

Most of these writers lay it down that criticism must ultimately be concerned with 'values.' No doubt; but who is to set the standard of value? Each critic, each layman, has his own standard, and to attempt to arrive at a universally valid scale of

values on these terms is like trying to work out a universally
serviceable scale of weights and measures when each man is
allowed to decide for himself how many ounces shall go to the
pound, or to say that two pounds of apples are not equal in
weight to two pounds of pears because he likes pears but does
not like apples. My complaint against musical criticism is that
it is still an almost childishly dilettantish thing; its general
incompetence was sufficiently shown by its utter inability to
find any basic principles to guide its practice when a problem
like the 'new' music was suddenly sprung upon it a few years
ago. Musical criticism has no principles, and has not as yet
even distilled any lessons from the past. As a humble but
inquiring practitioner of it, then, I submit that it is time we
critics gave up attempting the higher flights of the art and
began to learn how to walk. I am not suggesting that any of us,
critic or man in the street, should give up expressing his
opinions on music and musicians. I merely submit that the
bulk of this sort of writing is not worthy of the name of criticism.
It is only the expression of a personal temperamental reaction,
and therefore of no great interest to anyone but the writer of it.
It is simply a form of naive self-expression. As I have already
said, I long ago gave up reading 'musical criticism,' except
when compelled to do so for professional purposes, because
most of it tells me more about the critic than it does about the
composer; and it is in the composer that I am chiefly interested.

The only composer who has been at all adequately studied
is Beethoven, the reason being that only in his case have we
sufficient documents (his Sketch Books are particularly
valuable) that throw light on the structure of his musical
faculty. But even the mind of Beethoven still holds many
mysteries for us. Personally I have no further use for the kind
of Beethoven criticism that ranges in merely literary fashion
over his music, telling us, with more or less eloquence, how that
music has affected the writer, and setting forth the philosophy
of life it has engendered in the writer, which philosophy, of
course, he innocently proceeds to attribute to Beethoven himself. My contention is that three-fourths of what is written about
Beethoven is 'literature,' not music. Misled by this or that story
from his life, our writers read something into the music that is

not really there. They would never have discovered, or thought they had discovered, these things had all records of Beethoven's life perished the day he died. They form a certain conception of him from the story of his life, and then innocently proceed to foist that conception upon his music. They explain certain procedures of his music, certain episodes in it, on 'poetic' lines; whereas had they devoted a more intensive study to what I call the physiology of the music they would have found that these procedures, these episodes, were dictated to him not by this or that 'poetic' purpose but by the very nature of the constitution of his musical faculty. Think of all the rhapsodical nonsense, for example, that has been written about the 'Eroica'—simply because circumstances have put the idea of a hero into the writer's heads; yet a physiology of Beethoven's style would show that in the 'Eroica' he is merely obeying certain *musical* impulses that are so fundamental in him as to be equally apparent, on analysis, in most other works of his early and middle period.

There is so much humble spade-work to be done along these lines—the discovery of the basic unconscious principles upon which the composer's musical faculty has worked (and in no two composers are they the same)—that I can no longer have any patience with the criticism that indulges in mere literary rhapsody over the 'message' of the music; for in so far as this is not founded on an intimate understanding of the man's mind *as* a mind it is bound to be ill-informed, bound either to read into the music things that are not really there, or, if they are really there, to explain them in terms of literature rather than in terms of music.

Let me give a very simple example. Everyone knows the story of how certain repeated notes in one of Chopin's works represent the dropping of that rain that so affected the composer's nerves during his residence in Majorca; and it is difficult for any of us now, so familiar has the story been to us since our childhood, not to think of the raindrops when we listen to this Prelude. But to anyone with the slightest sense of a physiology of Chopin's style it is evident that repeated notes are one of the finger-prints of that style. They point to some sort of obsession that was rooted in the very sub-soil of his *musical* nature; and it

25

is the merest literary dilettantism to suppose that in a particular work it was the outcome of a particular external suggestion. If the repeated notes in this Prelude are the transcript of Chopin's thoughts as he listened one day to the rain, the only conclusion I can come to is that he must have written an extraordinarily large proportion of his music on wet days!

That may serve as an elementary illustration of the absurdity of looking for extra-musical reasons for certain procedures in a composer that are really the result of his peculiar *musical* construction; but I venture to say that it is intrinsically no more absurd than much of what has been written about the 'Eroica,' which Beethoven wrote in the precise way he did not because of the 'hero' concept but because of certain sub-conscious laws in his purely musical faculty.

I have already cited the case of Berlioz as one that especially needs examination from the point of view of a physiology of style. As yet there is hardly anything that deserves the name of Berlioz criticism. I am not concerned at the moment with whether people 'like' or 'dislike' his music; that is a matter for the individual. What I wish to suggest is that criticism, faced as it is here with the problem of a composer whose mind obviously works along lines very different from those of other composers, has not even made the beginning of an attempt to find out, by an analysis of his style, what it is that differentiates him from others. Not only is he judged by standards that do not apply to him, but he is played in a way that flouts his intentions. A little while ago I listened by wireless to a Continental performance of 'L'Enfance du Christ.' In the trio for two flutes and harp, Berlioz's phrase-markings were persistently ignored. The very essence of his rhythm is that it has the minimum of connection with the squareness of period that is really a derivation from folksong and dance. The fact that on the occasion to which I am referring the flute players consciously or unconsciously mistranslated his irregular periods into the four-square of ordinary music was a startling demonstration of how profoundly Berlioz's mind is misunderstood. How much of the ordinary criticism of his music is the result of the critic's unconscious application to it of standards that do not apply to it? And before a criticism of Berlioz is attempted ought not the critic at any rate to try to make sure that he is seeing the music as Berlioz himself saw it, not as Mozart or Brahms or Wagner would have seen it? And how is this elementary knowledge of Berlioz to be obtained without a preliminary study of the physiology of his musical faculty?

But I must stop. I still have no hope that I have made my meaning clear to the reader, but, like him, I feel, after four wearisome articles on the one subject, the need for a change of theme.

SKINNERISM: A DISEASE OF CRITICISM

28th February 1937

A LITTLE while ago, in my notice of some concert or other at which Mozart's D minor piano concerto had been played, I said something about the triviality and repetitiven. of the slow movement of that work, a movement which has always seemed to me very inferior to the first and third. This innocent remark of mine brought me some interesting letters: the following may be taken as typical of them. 'Dear Sir, Surely you are unusually harsh when you wrote last week of the Romanze in Mozart's D minor concerto? Admittedly the movement is inferior to the first, but then so is the third. .... I cannot see why this work has assumed an outstanding popularity to the exclusion of all the other [Mozart] concertos, if one third of it consists of 'repetitive trivialities.' Mozart himself thought highly of this concerto; it was probably Beethoven's favourite; and in my case the supreme pleasure this Romanze gives at the first two or three hearings will surely make up for any later disappointments.'

This is an admirably instructive example of what I would call Skinnerism—the tendency to see more than there really is in an acknowledged master's music as a whole, merely because he *is* an acknowledged master. I derive the term Skinnerism from the Miss Skinner of Samuel Butler's 'Way of All Flesh', who was in the happy position of being able to swallow Beethoven whole. Ernest Pontifex, it will be remembered, had confessed that he did not like Beethoven. 'I used to think I did, when I was younger, but I know now that I never really liked him.' 'Ah! how can you say so?' Miss Skinner replies. 'You cannot understand him, you never could say this if you understood him. For me a single chord of Beethoven is enough. This is happiness.' And with his inner ear Ernest seems to hear her saying to herself:

'Stay:
I may presently take
A simple chord of Beethoven,
or a small semiquaver
From one of Mendelssohn's Songs Without Words.'

The victim of this disease exhibits some strange symptoms. He has an acute eye for weaknesses or faults in a work so long as it is the work of a composer of the second or third order, or perhaps simply a composer who does not happen to strike on his box; on the other hand, the occasional faults or weaknesses of a first-rank or favourite composer impinge merely on his blind spot. Sometimes, it is true, he cannot evade a suspicion that his idol has slipped for a moment; but even then he extends a tolerance to the great man which he would not extend to a smaller one, and finds sophistical excuses for him which he would never think of putting forward in the other case. We are all of us, to some degree and at some time or other, sufferers from this disease. I suppose it has its origin in superabundance of love, and in our natural disinclination to admit a fault in the loved one: as Barry Pain put it once, if a girl is in love with a young man there is nothing he can do that she won't condone: let him steal the pennies out a of blind man's tin to buy poison for his grandmother, and the girl will say that it's just the boy's high spirits.

Let the reader look a little more closely at my correspondent's letter. He admits that the second movement is 'inferior to the first'; he as good as admits that the 'supreme pleasure' the Romanze gave him 'at the first two or three hearings' has not lasted; he even hints at 'later disappointments'. Admitting all this, he can still say I am 'unduly harsh' towards the movement! He rides off on an irrelevancy —the popularity of the concerto. But surely the high esteem in which the work as a whole is held is due in the main to the great first movement and the delightful third; many a listener puts up resignedly with the much weaker middle movement because he gets so much pleasure out of the other two. We have no right, that is to say, to speak of 'this concerto' as if it were an organic whole: it is merely a work in three movements, one of which is sombre and powerful, one exquisitely light-fingered, and one that is decidedly inferior to the other two.

Although I put it in that way, of course I am not asking the reader to accept my own valuation of the Romanze. I am content to leave matters of that kind to the individual: all I am concerned with is the element of Skinnerism in a good many of our valuations; and that element is something that deeply concerns the problem of criticism. Whether we are conscious of it or not, a great man's general greatness spreads a protective mantle over weaknesses in him that would alienate or chill us in the case of a smaller man. The mighty Bach can be, on occasion, devastatingly dull and mechanical; but the average listener, knowing that he is in the company of the mighty Bach, is reluctant to admit the dullness. Were the same work or the same movement to be submitted to him under the name of some contemporary of Bach of whom he knows nothing—Buxtehude or Ahle, for instance—he would frankly admit to himself that he was being bored; and conversely, if some reasonably good work by Reinken or Buxtehude that had been universally but wrongly attributed to Bach were put before him with the latter's name attached to it he would find all the typically Bachian virtues in it. In no art is it so true as it is in music that one man dare not look over the hedge while another can steal the horse and get away with it.

The most critical listener is apt to be the dupe of prepossessions or prejudices of this kind. I have been told that on one occasion Caruso, for the pure fun of the thing, sang the behind-the-scenes serenade of Harlequin in 'I Pagliacci', although the name of another tenor appeared in the programme as the player of the part. The result was just what one might have expected, and what Caruso had declared in advance it would be. No one, not even the critics, took any particular notice of his singing of the song. We are all of us predisposed to see what we expect to see, to hear what we expect to hear; and no one in the house that evening had expected anything remarkable in the singing of the serenade, no one heard anything remarkable in it. Now and then even the critics, who as a rule are infallible, as they would be the first to admit, fall down badly when they have to deliver a verdict without knowing just who the defendant is. When Mahler was at Leipzig he produced a reconstructed version of his own of Weber's unfinished opera 'Die drei Pintos': the critics praised, as pure Weber, certain things that Mahler himself had written, and censured, as merely an inexpert imitation of Weber's style by Mahler, certain other things which the latter had taken from unfamiliar works by Weber himself.

Let a violin concerto be brought out under Mozart's name and the unsuspecting public delight in it as pure Mozart: it is only when the experts throw doubts on the authenticity of the work that the listener in turn begins to have his doubts whether, after all, it is such good music as he had formerly imagined. Had the 'Jena' symphony which was discovered a few years ago come down to us with Beethoven's own signature on the manuscript, the lives of Beethoven would have been full of demonstrations of the importance of the work in a study of his development: but as the ascription of the symphony to Beethoven rests on nothing more substantial, so far as external evidence is concerned, than his name on one of the violin parts, no one quite knows what to make of it or what to say about it. It certainly *might* be by Beethoven; and, as Professor Fritz Stein, the discoverer of the parts from which the work has been put together, pertinently asks, if Beethoven did not write it who was the unknown who, in that epoch, could produce anything so good, and why have we not other works of his? It is all of no use: the world will never be able to decide whether the symphony is the work of a budding genius or merely one of the crowd until it knows for certain whether Beethoven or someone else wrote it. Then, of course, the question of its aesthetic value will be settled once for all, in accordance with the best principles in Skinnerism.

It is André Gide, I think, though I cannot lay my hand on the passage at the moment, who has raised the question whether some of the famous things in literature are really all they are cracked up to be, or whether we crack them up as we do because they come to us so festooned with conventional admiration that we are now almost incapable of seeing them as they actually are. He compares them to the toe of the statue of St Peter in Rome, that owes its present smoothness not to the original art of the sculptor but to the million kisses of the faithful. How much really second-rate music from the great masters, I wonder, do we admire as we do only because of the accumulated kisses of the accumulated Miss Skinners of the last few generations?

PART II

OPERA AND OPERA SINGERS

ACTORS AND ACTRESSES IN OPERA

7th March 1920

THE general rule in this world that women have the easier time than men may be seen to be operative even in opera. (I disclaim any intention of making a pun; the matter is too grave for levity.) It may be said broadly that the men have to *act* in opera, while the women have not—or, at least, no more than they do in the ordinary daily round of things. When one surveys the operatic field, indeed, one is astonished to find how very few real female character-studies there are in opera. The bulk of the women parts are pure convention.

Female characters in opera fall, for the most part, into three types—injured innocence (Elsa, Madam Butterfly, Desdemona, Verdi's Leonora, etc., etc., etc.), the hoyden or the soubrette (Musetta, Susanna, etc., etc., etc.), or the serpent of sex, crushing men in her folds or stinging them to the heart (terrible creatures these: Delilah, Carmen, Lola, etc., etc., etc.). Now it takes no great ability to play parts like these, because they are parts that, in varying degrees, women are playing in private all their lives through. All they have to do on the stage, in parts such as these, is to be themselves, be natural.

It may be objected that if any woman can do this sort of thing merely *qua* woman, there ought to be any number of good Carmens and Delilahs, whereas they are so scarce—especially the Carmens—that they can almost be counted, in any decade, on the fingers of one hand. But that is simply because Carmen and Delilah demand certain definite physical and vocal as well as mental gifts in the actress, and, owing to Nature's well-known habit of never doing a thing thoroughly where singers are concerned, it is rarely that we find all the necessary gifts combined in the same individual. Carmens are born, not made; and no amount of intelligence or of training will make a woman a Carmen if she is not born to it. She must be young, good-looking (and good-looking in a certain style), shapely, lithe,

35

electric, and with a voice of the right timbre. If she does not suggest the South, not merely in her make-up but in the rich, dark resonance of her voice, if she does not naturally 'go swinging upon her haunches', as Mérimée said of the original Carmen, 'like a filly from the Andalusian stables', she is not Carmen at all.

So, in the other direction, with Mélisande. Any woman can act injured innocence; but for Mélisande's particular sort, an actress needs a certain shape, a certain physique, a certain look, and a certain timbre of voice; and the combination of all the gifts in the one woman is rare. 'The whole man thinks', said George Henry Lewes. 'The whole man (or woman) sings', we may hear. Let me hear anyone sing, and I will tell you what he or she is. The life's habits, the life's experiences, are betrayed in the voice. There are voices that of themselves, their mere timbre, independently of what they are singing, suggest the high-minded man of culture. Such a voice is that of Mr Gervase Elwes. There are some fine voices (fine from the purely vocal point of view) that can only be called brainless. Such are the voices of Mr ——, Signor ——, and Madame ——. (The friends of these singers can fill in the names under their breath.) A Mélisande voice, like a Carmen voice, will not be found in one operatic artist in a hundred.

There are, it is true, some genuine female character studies in opera—Norma, Beethoven's Leonora, Brynhilde, Elektra, Salome, and one or two more—and women of genius have made tremendous things of them. Here they genuinely *act*; that is to say, they really, by an effort of the dramatic imagination, and in virtue of a fine technique, get within the skin of a character that is not simply themselves. But on the whole, women have very little acting to do in opera, because, as I have said, to play the injured innocent, the hoyden, or the temptress is, for women, not acting at all. It is curious how often they fail in what should be the easiest things to a genuine actress. The other evening, for instance, Miss Nelis, as Cherubino, sang as charmingly as she looked; but there was no suggestion of the boy about her except the costume. The singing was purely feminine singing; whereas the voice ought all the time to suggest an adolescent boy, not merely a girl in boy's clothes; and this new timbre would surely come for the moment into the voice of any actress who had really hypnotised herself into imagining she was a boy.

Even when women get a chance to lift a character out of the conventional psychological rut they cannot do it. Now and then a librettist gives them such a chance by pure inadvertence. I have elsewhere pointed out that Delilah, for one brief moment, fails to be true to type. It is where she refuses the High Priest's offer of gold and jewels for the seducing of Samson. One can hardly imagine a lady of her profession refusing riches; a Delilah who did would no doubt be struck off the rolls of her few fellow practitioners for unprofessional conduct. But the incident, at any rate, gives the actress a chance to lend a touch of originality to her playing of the part. They all pass it over, however, as a harmless eccentricity on the part of the librettist; they take the easier course of making Delilah just the conventional temptress of melodrama. Some day, perhaps, a contralto who has read Meredith will give us a suggestion of Mrs Mount in her Delilah; then we shall call her an actress.

Men, on the other hand, have some difficult tasks to perform. They have to be characters, not types. Any intelligent schoolgirl with a good voice could play Desdemona; but only a great actor can play Othello, especially as Mr Mullings* plays it. And in some parts the man has to put in more than the librettist and the composer ever dreamed of in order to give the character some sort of interest. Mr Mullings's genius the other evening gave us a Tannhäuser that was quite incredible but intensely interesting. Wagner's Tannhäuser is either an ass or a prig. No one but an ass would prefer Elizabeth to Venus, or the solemn bores and noodles of the Wartburg to the ballet of the Venusberg. No one but a prig would pretend that he did. Mr Mullings makes Tannhäuser a man of such fine intellect that we can only wonder how he could ever have lived a year with the Landgrave and the rest of the pious dullards without despising them from the bottom of his heart, or how he could

*Frank Mullings, former British tenor, whose great reputation dates from his appearances with the Beecham Opera Company and the British National Opera Company, was one of the most famous English interpreters of Otello and Tristan. Died May, 1953.

ever have supposed it necessary to his peace of mind that the Pope should approve of him.

To play Tannhäuser as Wagner conceived him, a tenor should be rather stupid and illiterate. Mr Mullings is a reader and a thinker, and he cannot divest himself of his twentieth century culture; so he makes this piece of tiresome mediaeval nonsense so intellectual as to be quite incredible. But what genius it takes to carry the incredibility through as he does it! When I see some woman singer turn librettist and composer out of doors in the same way, and re-make a conventional part in her own image, I shall acclaim her as a great actress.

THE MODERN ENGLISH SONG

2nd May 1920

IT is natural that in the present renaissance of English music the smaller forms should play the larger part, for the chances of performance are all in favour of the smaller works. It is this factor, as much as any other, that accounts for our having seemingly made not much progress, compared with ten years ago, in orchestral music and the opera, while there has been notable progress in chamber music, the song, and music for the pianoforte alone. It is in the song, I think, that, on the whole, we have travelled furthest during the last few years. It is not that we have yet discovered the master, the English Schubert, Schumann, Brahms, Wolf, or Moussorgsky. But we are at least producing a number of quite good songs each year that show, for the most part, a refreshing absence of anything like a family likeness.

This dissimilarity is a welcome sign that no British composer who is worth his salt cares two straws whether he is writing in a 'national' style or not. Any attempt to create a 'national' British idiom on the basis of British folk-song could only lead to merely imitative, and therefore insincere, work. Nothing finally matters in art but the personality of the artist. He may work within a tradition, national or local, as the German composers do in one way, and some composers who have founded their style on folk-music have done in another; but not even the best tradition will help a bad composer to write like a good one. We may call a composer like Granados or Albeniz a 'national' Spanish composer, or a composer like Moussorgsky a 'national' Russian composer, if we have a passion for using words in this loose way, simply because he draws more or less liberally on the stereotyped rhythms or melodic turns of his country or his province; but there are always hundreds of composers doing this sort of thing at the same time without one of them being a Granados, an Albeniz, or a Moussorgsky.

But even this way of working is impossible to an Englishman. We have nothing in the nature of a 'national' rhythm, for instance, corresponding to the Spanish rhythms that Albeniz and Granados exploit so successfully. An English song composer, then, must rely even more than a Russian or a Spaniard on his own personality alone. And it is gratifying to see that our modern song writers are doing this. An evening of modern English song has nothing of the monotony, for instance, of an evening of Czechoslovak song. We do not get the same recipes served up again and again; there are, generally speaking, as many styles and idioms as there are composers. At Miss Olga Haley's recital the other evening there were some twenty British composers represented; and though it cannot be said that all of them were heaven-sent geniuses, each of them, at any rate, went about the business in his own way.

Before I deal with what I take to be the main reasons for the failures of so much honest endeavour, and frequently so much fine musicianship in the British song, let me say a friendly, if critical, word to the recitalists. Some of these, in their anxiety to help on the cause of British music, are not as particular as they might be in their choice of songs. They are often too willing to include a song merely because it is British; their idea is that even if the song is not first-rate the performance of it will encourage the composer to do better, and will widen the field of opportunity for the British composer in general. I venture to think they are labouring under a delusion. You cannot turn a poor composer into a good one by encouraging him. Whatever his powers, we may be sure that, in general, he always does his best; and if this or that specimen of his best is poor, there is no earthly reason why anyone should be put to the trouble of performing it or any audience to the pain of listening to it.

In art the ideal critical ethic is ruthlessness. There the race is only to the fleet and the battle to the strong. There should be no thought of helping lame dogs—and still less sick or deformed dogs—over the stile; if the dog is going to be as helpless the other side of the stile as he is on this side, then let him stay on this side till he is strong enough to get over by himself. He is no worse off, while you have saved yourself a good deal of trouble (perhaps a biting also), and may have spared the people on the other side the infliction of a nuisance on them. The practice of art should not be made easier for the weaklings; it should be made harder, so that only the best types may survive.

It is for this reason that I am unrepentant in the matter of my strictures on the British Music Society for having wasted so many pages of its annual on the lists of the complete works of so many utterly unimportant composers. A publication of this sort, that is designed to help the cause of British music abroad, ought to put up an extra high fence against inferior work. A foreign Lieder singer, let us suppose, having heard so much about the renaissance of our music, feels that he would like to include a few British songs in his next programme. He naturally turns to the lists in the British Music Society's Annual. He looks out for the specialists in song. He finds a page and a half devoted to the songs of Mr Montague Phillips, and another two pages or so to the songs of Mr Eric Coates. 'Ah', he says to himself, 'one of these gentlemen, no doubt, is the English Hugo Wolf, otherwise he would not have devoted himself so largely to song writing, and would not be held in such reverence by the British Music Society.' So he orders a few dozen of the songs of Mr Phillips and Mr Coates, and after reading through 'Sweet Eyes of Blue', 'The Beat of a Passionate Heart', 'Were I a Moth', 'Love's Spell', 'The Little Girl I Love', 'Your Heart is Like a Garden Fair', 'Rose of Mine', 'Land of My Heart', My Prayers Take Wings to Find You', 'The Heart You Love is Calling', and a few more masterpieces of the sort, he asks himself if this is the English music of whose renaissance he hears so much, and begins to wonder whether it is he or the compilers of the British Music Society's Annual who ought to be put in a padded room. So with the singers of British songs. If they want to do their country's music a service, let them keep out of their programmes every song that their artistic conscience does not assure them is really good; for there is no knowing into whose innocent hands, here or abroad, a programme may fall.

41

SPECIALISATION IN SINGING

4th June 1922

SPECIALISATION seems to have extended by now to most things except music: the musical critic, for instance, is expected to be an authority on everything—to see another and yet another point in Bach's soul unseized by the Germans yet, to know the difference between a trumpet and a tromba marina, and to be able to criticise performances of all sorts of music that he has never studied, on all sorts of instruments that he cannot play. I can foresee the time when there will be no scope for such dangerous omniscience, when the musical critic will be as severely specialised as the machine hands in a factory. The day will yet come when the critic of the *Times* will be recognised as *the* authority on the G string, and when, for a reasoned estimate of the middle notes of a new tenor, we shall turn instinctively to the musical column of the *Daily News*.

But before that happy day comes we shall reach, no doubt, some sort of specialisation among singers. We do not expect a violinist to play a 'cello concerto on his small instrument: but —in this country at any rate—we expect a singer to execute any and every kind of music regardless of the size or the quality of his voice. There is no attempt at classification. I have seen a tomtit tenor break his little bill against music that was intended for a great auk: I have heard sopranos and contraltos whose whole charm came from the devil they had in them try vainly to represent saints and angels in our oratorios. To-night a tenor is expected to sing Julian, tomorrow Faust, a day or two later Siegfried or Tristan: while next week he will try his hand at the Narrator's recitatives in the Matthew Passion, and the week after that give a recital of songs of all nations, all periods, all styles.

With all respect, it simply cannot be done, except perhaps by one genius in ten thousand. The ordinary good singer can no more succeed in every style than the ordinary healthy man can shine at every game. In civilised countries this principle is broadly recognised. An opera singer is an opera singer, a

Lieder singer is a Lieder singer; a heroic tenor is a heroic tenor, and would not be asked to sing puling ballads about 'You'; a lyrical tenor is a lyrical tenor, and would not be expected to sing Othello. That is because in those happy countries there is enough music of all sorts, and enough singers of all sorts, to permit of specialisation.

Here there is so little of either sort that a singer has to be prepared to take anything that may turn up, whether it suits him or not. The native German or Italian specialist is so good in his own line that we make it no reproach against him that he cannot hopefully attempt any other; we would not expect a Caruso, for example, to be impressive in a Hugo Wolf programme. But in England a singer is expected to do everything: and the frequent result of his trying to succeed in twenty styles is that he fails in them all.

Students are taught too much in the abstract. We would not train a boxer and a golfer on identical principles; yet the same sort of vocal training is supposed to fit a young man or woman to sing either Wagner or Ivan Caryll. Occasionally an example from abroad comes to show us the absurdity of this abstract culture: an Italian tenor, with a purely Italian voice, a purely Italian method, and a purely Italian outlook will sing Wagner or Moussorgsky, and we have to hold our sides with laughter. Only recently Chaliapine's almost comical failures in German songs proved that *his* methods are purely Russian, and should be reserved for Russian music.

It is true that very intelligent and adaptive singers can accommodate themselves pretty well to the various national and personal styles in music; but singers of this type are rare. And of course they solve their problem by first recognising that there *is* a problem to be solved; whereas the ordinary English student is never warned that singing is full of problems. He is turned out of his conservatoire with a sort of reach-me-down 'production' that is supposed to be appropriate wear for all occasions. He will then sing, for the rest of his career, Wagner, Puccini, Moussorgsky, Debussy, and Elgar with precisely the same tones and the same verbal inflections, oblivious of distinctions of personal style, of national tradition, and of language.

43

The bulk of the unsatisfactory singing we are now getting in the 'Ring' comes from this failure on the part of the average singer to realise that Wagner simply cannot be sung just like Gounod or Montague Phillips. We cannot justly quarrel with these good people for mostly having voices much too small for their parts: that is not their fault. But it *is* their fault, or that of their teachers, that they have never asked themselves whether the 'Ring' has a musical style of its own, and tried to find out what that style is. They have apparently not realised the first principle of this style—that the consonants are of prime importance. When their words are inaudible, as they mostly are, they are told by indulgent critics that after all the words do not greatly matter, the music being the thing.

I should have liked to hear anyone say that to Wagner, and listened to the irate composer's reply, which would probably have been that he objected to being called a fool. For that is what this theory of the words not mattering amounts to. Not only do they matter in the most obvious sense of all—for they carry the characters and the drama on their shoulders—they matter in the further sense that they are inextricably part and parcel of the melodic and rhythmic being of the music.

The alliteration of the 'Ring' is not merely a game on Wagner's part. It determines the structure of the vocal melodies; it supports them as the poles of a tent support the canvas. The ordinary English singer, trained to 'produce' his voice nicely, and thinking all the time of his tone, either does not see the importance of Wagner's often hard consonants or is resentful of them for getting in the way of his 'vocalisation'; so he softens them and smooths them out, not understanding that by so doing he breaks the back of Wagner's rhythm. Wagner had none of the Italian-trained singer's horror of harsh consonants: he revelled in the expressiveness of them when harshness was the very thing he wanted. The English singer, by toning down the harshness in the interests of what he imagines to be his singing, makes all Wagner's labour in vain. When Wagner made Alberich say, as he stumbles and slithers over the rocks, 'Garstig glatter glitschriger Glimmer! Wie gleit' ich aus!' he really meant it. He was not concerned to present Mr So-and-So's voice to the audience groomed and barbered: he wanted to suggest the stumbling and the slithering, and the irritation they were to Alberich's temper. The consonants must be insisted on. The English singer, by smoothing out the English equivalents of lines such as these because, as he says, they are not 'singable' (heaven help him!) gives us an Alberich that is about as like Wagner's Alberich as any white-waistcoated gentleman in the Covent Garden stalls is like the chimpanzee from which he sprang.

But it is not only in harshly graphic passages such as these that the singer's failure to appreciate the correspondence between Wagner's verbal accents and his music makes his singing a perversion of the essential Wagner style. Many of our 'Ring' singers have obviously no idea of the true build of their phrases, the peaks and valleys of the accentuation, the relation of phrase to phrase. They distribute their stresses wrongly: they take breath in the most absurd places. Some of the consequences are almost unendurably painful to the ear that knows its Wagner: in charity I refrain from giving specific instances. There have been times during this week's performance of the 'Ring' when I have regretted, not that some of the singers could be heard only with difficulty through the orchestra, but that they could be heard at all.

ACTING IN OPERA:

I

SOME SPECIAL DIFFICULTIES

16th June 1935

OUR friends the dramatic critics, on the rare occasions when they dignify the musical theatre with their presence, are inclined to be rather contemptuous of the acting they see there. I am afraid I cannot put up much of a defence for it, for most of it is appallingly bad. But at any rate I can in the first place try to explain the peculiar difficulties under which operatic acting labours and suggest the necessity of judging it by different standards from those of the spoken drama, and in the second place hurl a *tu quoque* in the teeth of the people who crack up the ordinary brand of acting at the expense of the operatic brand.

Much of what we see in the theatre is, in my humble opinion, not acting at all. It is excellent stuff of its kind, delivering the goods expected of it, and therefore, from the point of view of the evening's entertainment, wholly admirable. All I have to say against it is that we ought to try to find another name for it than acting. For acting means, surely, suggesting for the moment that you are someone else than your ordinary self. Tried by this standard, how many genuine actors or actresses have we? What happens, as a rule, is that an actress is discovered to have a gift for revealing, without the slightest effort, some pleasing aspect of a personality, and then she is regularly cast for parts that enable her to display this one gift: the titles of the characters are changed from play to play, from film to film, but the character itself remains virtually the same throughout. I do not call being yourself acting, in the fullest and most honourable sense of the word; and so I cannot regard the famous Miss This or the eminent Mr That as very much of an actor. But I would call Mr Nelson Keys an actor,

46

because over a very wide field he gives us, for the moment, the conviction that he is someone else than the man he is when he walks down the Strand.

We have it on the highest journalistic authority that if a dog bites a man, that's nothing, but if a man bites a dog, that's news. On the same lines we may say that if Carnera were to play Goliath, that would be nothing; but if Tom Thumb were to play Goliath in such a way as to make us feel that, in spite of the handicap of his stature, there came over to us for the moment the mentality of Goliath, that would be acting. The illustration, of course, taken literally is absurd, because the natural distance between the two poles of effort and possibility is too great: but we have only to bring the poles step by step nearer to each other to see what acting really means, or ought to mean. If Mr Smith, in virtue of something suggestive of the underworld in his appearance, his manner, his accent, the timbre of his voice, his whole mentality, plays to perfection the part of a low-bred criminal, I enjoy his performance, but I still award him only a few marks as an actor. I would call him an actor, however, if he were to play Lord Chesterfield in such a way as to make me believe, for the time being, that he *was* Lord Chesterfield, not merely altering superficially his accent and so on, but suggesting to me that all his life he had moved in the politest and most cultured circles. How many actors of that kind or calibre have we?

Acting in the spoken drama, then, is rather rarer than most people imagine. I admit that it is still rarer in opera, and that for two reasons. In the first place the average opera singer receives no training worth mentioning in acting. All his time as a young man is spent in learning how to sing: once it is established that he has a voice he is shoved on the stage as Tristan or Figaro, and he picks up a few—very few, in most instances—routine tricks of the job as he goes along.

The problem is easier for the women, because so many leading female operatic parts are mere conventions that call for nothing more than the exploitation of the characteristics that make a woman what she is in private life. As I pointed out last week, any woman who is young enough, has a decent figure, has the right kind of voice, knows how to use it, and is not an absolute

47

fool, simply cannot fail to give us a passable Carmen, Mimi, or Delilah. Mimi, indeed, is the easiest of all operatic parts for a young person with a pleasant voice and a youthful figure. So I remain critically unmoved when that sort of young person plays Mimi: paradoxical as it may seem, I am much more interested when a middle-aged lady who weighs in at fourteen stone tries her hand at Mimi, for then, if she has any gift at all as an actress, I am interested in the spectacle of the constant conflict between her art and her handicap, and am the more ready to give her credit when the former is triumphant.

Male singers have open to them none of these easy parts in which all the man has to do is to be himself. No Smith or Brown or Robinson of them all is really a Tristan, a Lohengrin, a Don José, or an Almaviva. To play any one of these parts convincingly he has to be an actor; and whether he has any natural capacity for acting or not, as a rule he has had practically no training in the actor's art. The result is the sticks that stalk about the stage in opera houses, and command large salaries for doing so.

In the second place, opera imposes peculiar disabilities on the actor. As a rule, opera is given in very large theatres, where subtle facial expression, even if it exists, has much less chance of getting across than facial expression has in a smaller theatre. Further, it is very difficult at once to mould the face according to the psychological requirement of the moment, *and* sing. Singing, in the main, is what might be called a whole-time job for any human face. You can convince yourself of this by watching the Italian singers in a Rossini opera. In the recitatives, some of them display considerable gifts as actors; their movements and gestures are varied and expressive, and their faces reflect the meaning of what they are saying. The moment they break into an aria, however, they become just singing machines, with faces like putty and with no resource in the way of gesture but a few conventional motions of the arms. The man is no longer an actor: he is merely a mouth emitting sounds.

Moreover, the operatic singer is far more restricted than the the ordinary actor in his or her choice of parts. A singer may have all the mental and physical qualifications for playing Isolde or Brynhilde; but if her voice happens to be of the wrong range and timbre she has to be satisfied all her life with Brangaene and Fricka; and so ad infinitum. The result is that the operatic stage is packed with psychological misfits, to say nothing of the fact that, in many cases, if an operatic singer has a voice he has no brains, while the best brains will not of themselves produce the right kind of tone or the right power of tone for the opening cry of Otello if the voice is not there. In a hundred respects the odds are against first-rate acting in opera. Still, a great deal more could be done than is done at present; and if the reader can stand this boring subject for another week I will try next Sunday to suggest what might be done.

II

HOW IT MIGHT BE IMPROVED

23rd June 1935

LAST week I suggested that there is comparatively little now in the ordinary theatre that an actor or a playgoer of a couple of generations ago would have dignified with the name of acting. When we read that the production of this or that new play is 'a triumph of casting' we can be tolerably sure that what has happened is that the players have been chosen simply to exploit once more, in other circumstances, some personal characteristic or other with which they have become associated in the public mind, and that calls for the minimum of real acting on their part. It was not so in the old days, when actors were, and had to be, actors—that is to say, a different person-ality in each part they undertook. Today, largely owing to the coming of the films, we find that one man in his time plays not many parts but the same part over and over again. Nature having endowed Mr Blotto, for instance, with a face that suggests an amiable rabbit whose brains were removed some time before birth, he is in great demand to play silly-ass parts: the part for which he is cast is specially built up to go with his face, and all he has to do is to look like and to be himself.

We are approaching a situation of this kind in the operatic world, where the repertory of the most popular singers seems to be contracting every year. The repertory of both actors and singers was much wider in the past. We are astonished at the number and the range of the parts played, for example, by Emil Devrient, the greatest German actor of about the middle of the nineteenth century. And the singers who nowadays trot all over the globe singing nothing but the same four or five Wagner parts for ever and ever seem pretty poor specimens compared with Lilli Lehmann, whose repertory ran to nearly 120 parts of every imaginable kind, Adam, Bellini, Auber, Beethoven, Dittersdorf, Wagner, Verdi, Donizetti, Offenbach, Suppé, and a score of others being equally within her scope.

We shall have to accept as the normal thing in the future, I am afraid, this limitation of the operatic singer to a very small range of parts. Wagner saw from the beginning that each national and each personal style in opera calls for its own kind of singing and acting: Bayreuth came into being, indeed, primarily from the necessity of training singers whose style had become a bad mixture of all styles in the style specifically appropriate to his own music and dramatic ideals. And since our singers are severely restricted in their choice of parts by the range, the timbre, and the power of their voices, the only thing to do now seems to be to let them specialise to their hearts' content, but also to insist on their securing for themselves, and passing on to their listeners, the full value of this specialisation. If the acting singer is going to play on only one instrument all his life, we have at least the right to demand that he shall play on it with thorough competence. A pianist who played Couperin in precisely the same style as Liszt would be regarded as hardly having thought out much more than the rudiments of his job. The case is not much better when the operatic actor plays upon his voice in precisely the same way in parts of the most diverse kinds.

Let me give a concrete example. A singer whom we all know and admire greatly has been endowed by nature with a great gift for pathetic expression through her voice alone, its peculiarly moving timbre, its delicate inflections. This natural formula, for such we may call it, fits almost magically such a part as that of the Marschallin in the 'Rosenkavalier', the part of a woman whose pathos resides in her consciousness of the gradual slipping away of her youth. But when exactly the same formula of vocal expression is applied to Sieglinde, then, however moving the singer's accents may be in themselves, we feel that it is the operatic artist, rather than Sieglinde, to whom we are listening—that the pathos of Sieglinde should have a different, a bigger, more saga-like quality about it. The pathos of Elsa is, or should be, of another kind again—the pathos of a woman much younger and less consciously sorry for herself than the Marschallin, of a woman, again, whose yet unawakened nature has never had to face the realities of life as Sieglinde has had to do. To sing, therefore, Elsa's famous 'Mein armer Bruder!' with precisely the same timbre, the same accents, the same inflections, the same consequent psychological suggestions, as are employed for the Marschallin of the end of the first act of the 'Rosenkavalier' or the Sieglinde of the second act of the 'Valkyrie', is, it seems to me, to achieve, with the best intentions, merely a sort of dramatic falsity. I may add that to import the same unvarying formula of expression into one German Lied after another is to carry the process of psychological misrepresentation still further.

One way, then, in which operatic singers could improve their acting—that is to say, the verisimilitude of their suggestion of the character of the moment—would be to learn to play more subtly than they do now upon their voices, to modify their natural formulae to suit the requirements of each part or each situation. That the thing is not impossible has been proved by Chaliapine.

Since much play of facial expression is difficult, if not impossible, when one is singing, the operatic actor should concentrate on expressive facial play and gesture when he is not singing. The finest acting I saw at Covent Garden this year was that of Mme Ohms* as Ortrud. Unfortunately, however, highly intelligent work of this kind is apt to go unnoticed by the main body of the audience, because of the tendency to keep one's eyes on the singer of the moment, to

*Elizabeth Ohms, former Dutch soprano, was for many years a member of the Munich opera. She appeared at Covent Garden between 1928 and 1935 in Wagnerian rôles.

the neglect of everyone else. The result, in the case I have just mentioned, was that while the Lohengrin or the Elsa of the evening was doing nothing at all out of the common in the first two acts—merely singing, indeed, more or less well—and the real drama as Wagner conceived it was being carried almost entirely on the shoulders of Mme Ohms, few people had eyes for her. We are, in fact, up against one of the fundamental disabilities attached to opera—the curious attraction the person who happens to be singing at the moment has for the average spectator, to the neglect of something far more dramatically significant that may be going on elsewhere on the stage.

The best way to ensure that our opera singers shall act would be, of course, to insist on their going through a proper training in acting in their young days, when the body is flexible and teachable. But if the most we can expect of the majority of them is that they shall make the best use possible of a few standardised gestures and attitudes and movements, at all events let us insist on their exploiting these intelligently. The Russian Ballet has shown us that with virtually no facial play at all, and with the minimum of gesture, it is possible to convey a good deal in the way of psychological suggestion. But in the miming ballet the vital gesture or movement is carefully worked out to begin with, the incidence of it is accurately timed, and owing to the dancer's perfect control of his body he can hold it as long as is necessary. Theoretically something of this kind might be arranged for our opera singers: as so many of them have to have the words and the music of their parts drilled into them almost by force of arms, there could be no objection to their being similarly drilled in, or dragooned into, the art of elementary movement. But whether the theory could be widely converted into practice is perhaps doubtful: most of our famous or notorious singers would be taking up this study too late in life—you can't teach an old dog tricks!—and with bodies too set and too unwieldy for very much to be done with them. It would be interesting, however, some day to see an opera produced by singers whose bodies and minds had been properly taken in hand at the early age at which the ballet dancer begins to be trained for his career.

WHAT IS 'SINGING'?

I

LIEDER SINGING

14th February 1937

LAST week I raised the question whether there *is* such a thing as 'singing'—that is to say, singing *per se*. In the purely technical sense, of course, there is; singing means producing from the human throat a succession of tones at definite pitches; and good singing, so far as that definition is concerned, would simply mean producing tones that are beautiful in themselves and in perfect tune with each other and with the accompanying instrument.

Considering the matter even from that rudimentary point of view it is a sad fact that we seldom hear really good singing: at the best, an opera or concert performance, taking the singers *en masse*, is rarely more than fifty per cent. or so of the real thing, while at anything less than the best we get something that suggests that when Poe wrote (or might have written),

> . . . and their tongues can only speak
> In a tuneless jangling wrangling as they
> shriek, and shriek, and shriek,

he must have had some experience as a music critic: throughout how many performances, for instance, have I, for one, felt, with the poet of 'The Bells,' that

> There is neither rest nor respite, save the quiet of the tomb!

We hear extremely little good singing in the purely technical sense of the term; mercifully for us, our ears are so blunted by constantly listening to the second-rate that it is seldom we realise how far from the first-rate even eighty per cent. of the best singing is.

By 'singing', however, I do not mean, for my present purpose, simply voice production. Our concert and opera singers do not sing just for singing's sake—if they did, mere vowel sounds and notes in any order would do; nor do we in the audience listen to a performance with our interest wholly centred in singing for singing's sake. The singers have to reproduce for us, and make significant to us, what the composer had in his mind when he wrote his music; and since what the composer had in his mind means something quite different in each case, it is obvious that 'singing' in the full sense of the term means, or ought to mean, something quite different in each case. Everything depends on the nature of the music and of the words.

To begin with, there is a type of music in which the words count for practically nothing, while the music, being little more than the exploitation of a formula—the value of the music varying with the amount of genius the composer can turn upon the exploitation of the formula—calls for nothing more than good tone, good intonation, and good line. Take, by way of illustration, things like the two tenor arias in 'Don Giovanni'— 'Dalla sua pace' and 'Il mio tesoro.' The words are mere trash: most listeners have no idea what they mean, while for those who do know what they mean almost any other Italian words that would fit the melody would do equally well. The music, for its part, is concerned with nothing outside itself; it consists simply of notes following each other in agreeable melodic patterns. An aria of this kind demands nothing but good 'singing' in the simplest possible acceptation of that term. I do not mean by this that it is easy to sing. Far from it, as our sad experience has taught us! It calls for a first-rate voice and a first-rate vocal technique. In a thing of this sort the voice is used almost purely and simply as an instrument; and it is because so few singers have the quality and the skill of the ordinarily good instrumentalist that so few of them can make even a passable showing in this kind of music.

But even supposing an old-style Italian opera aria to be sung according to all the rules of the game, some listeners still find themselves unable to suppress the critical spirit. For the game itself is apt to reveal itself as too obviously a game. The singers of this kind of music all tend to do pretty much the same thing at the same points: the pattern has become established, and all they have to do is to reproduce it according to their individual powers. Hence it comes about that, apart from certain inevitable differences in vocal timbre, one Italian (or Italianised) tenor's singing of the Duke's opening aria in 'Rigoletto' is hardly distinguishable from another's. And because the style *is* constructed on a pattern, and the pattern is easily acquired by imitation, the tenors are inclined to do virtually the same thing in every set aria they have to sing; there is the same 'spinning' of the tone, the same standardised nuancing at the regulation points, the same manner of treating high notes, the same way of making an effect of climax, and so on. Further, because of this standardisation, an evening of that kind of singing leaves on the critical listener an impression of a certain intellectual limitation on the part of the singers. It is in the main *vox et praeterea nihil*; he leaves the theatre with the feeling that he has been assisting at the operatic equivalent of a dish that was popular with the old Roman epicures—nightingales' tongues and peacocks' brains.

Once more I must take care to guard myself against misunderstanding. I do not despise this kind of singing: when it is perfect of its type, it can give exquisite pleasure of a particular kind, the same kind of pleasure that we get from a fine instrumental performance. And there are people who look for no other pleasure but this from singing. The result is that they are inclined to judge other kinds of singing by a wrong criterion.

For there is another kind of *music* than the one that gave birth to this style and that finds its fullest realisation in it. There is a type of music that is shot through and through with poetic suggestion; and in this type, as the vocal line is determined by other than quasi-instrumental considerations, obviously the style appropriate to it is not that of what we may call purely instrumental singing. Each great song inhabits a mental world of its own: it follows, therefore, that the singer, if he wishes to carry us with him, must reproduce that world for us. Standardised methods will not do here, nor does a fine voice suffice of itself. Some of the very worst Lieder singing, in fact, is given us by people with voices that are admirably musical in the abstract. For here the abstract simply will not do. Some voices are fundamentally unfitted by their very nature

55

to express certain emotions or certain poetic ideas—a rudimentary fact which the ordinary Lieder singer is curiously slow to recognise when she makes up her programme.

It is perfectly useless for the soprano with a sweet crystalline voice to try to suggest spiritual shadow; yet singers with voices of this kind will pass without a break, and without a suspicion of the absurdity of the proceeding, from the Brahms 'Cradle Song' to the 'Sapphische Ode' or 'Immer leiser wird mein Schlummer', or from Wolf's delicate little 'Der Gärtner' to his 'Gebet' or 'Mühvoll komm' ich und beladen'. Further, both the technique and the musical understanding of most of our Lieder singers are too limited, too patternised, for them to be able either to give a particular song the vocal colour it requires or to grasp its essential rhythm. It is obvious, to take the latter point alone, that a song like Brahms's 'Der Schmied' calls for a peculiar incisiveness of rhythm—the kind of thing that Elena Gerhardt and Nikisch in combination used to achieve to perfection; yet the average singer and accompanist can do no more with the song than make its regular three-four sound like waltz-time.

It is because most recitalists persist in attempting Lieder for which they have neither the appropriate vocal colour nor the right musical and poetic understanding that the critic so often finds himself compelled to say that all the songs sounded very much alike, as if they had all been written by the same composer, or at any rate had come from the same epoch and milieu. And the worst possible judges of Lieder singing—or indeed, for that matter, of Lieder themselves—are the people whose sole standard of singing is the quasi-instrumental, the people who are fundamentally insensitive to that suffusion of music by poetry that is the very essence of the Lied in its most highly developed form. I have repeatedly been astonished to find people of this type expressing their delight in a performance that had seemed to me to be the last word in absurdity: they had been satisfied with the natural charm of the singer's voice, and blind to the fact that this purely physical charm had no organic relation whatever to what the poet and the composer were talking about. Per contra, I have known people of this type to be quite insensitive to a performance that had seemed to me to get to the very heart of the poetic and musical matter; *they* had missed in the performance the special virtues of what I have called singing in the abstract. The truth is that in musical practice there is no such thing as 'singing' *per se*. There are merely different styles of singing, severally appropriate to different kinds of music and words; and the critical standards applicable to one style are only to a very small degree applicable to the others.

Operatic singing is yet another matter. I shall devote my article to this subject next week.

II

OPERA SINGING

21st February 1937

IN my last week's article I dealt with the difference between 'instrumental' singing and Lieder singing: in the former the words count for nothing, the vital matter being beauty of tone, purity of intonation, and elegance of accent and phrasing: in Lieder singing the words, or rather what is at the back of the words, play a large part in determining the appropriate musical style. And not only does this style vary as between Lied and Lied, composer and composer, but the very timbre or weight of the voice has to be taken into consideration. A particular natural quality of voice that may be a great asset in the case of one song may be a hopeless liability in the case of another.

The difficulties of the opera singer are even greater than those of the Lieder singer, for he has to be an actor as well. For the imperfect performances we generally get in opera houses the singer is not always primarily to blame. Our friends the dramatic critics are apt to become satirical when they discuss acting in opera. Their strictures, however, are not wholly just. In the first place, 'acting' does not and cannot mean the same thing in the spoken drama and in opera: the opera singer's face, with the set of the mouth determined by the necessity for rounded tone production, cannot be expected to have the same mobility as the face of the actor who has only words to utter.

57

In the second place, the quick give-and-take, ebb-and-flow of spoken dialogue is impossible in music, which demands room in which to unfold itself.

In the third place—and this is the most vital point of all—the opera singer cannot pick and choose his parts as the ordinary actor can. No actor is cast for a part unless nature has already indicated him, physically and mentally, as a reasonable candidate for that part; but the opera singer has often to play parts for which nature has given him only one real qualification—the nature and the range of his voice. It is true that some half-dozen people can spend their lives trotting round the world singing for ever and ever the same four or five parts. But these are exceptions: the average tenor has to try his hand at all sorts of parts, in all sorts of opera, merely because he *is* a tenor. Is it to be wondered at that even if he can sing the music adequately (which is rarely the case), he often strikes us as a sorry misfit in the part as a whole? Nature may have given him a fine voice; but she has carelessly neglected to provide him with either the necessary appearance or the necessary mentality for many of the parts he is called upon to play.

And in opera the mentality is of considerable importance; if a singer says to us, in effect, 'Tonight I am Tristan, or Walther, or Isolde, or Brynhilde', we have the right to expect from him or her not merely the notes set down in the score, but the mind of the character as Wagner conceived it. If he or she is obviously not that character, the best singing in the world will not reconcile the thoughtful listener to the loss of so much that seems to him vital to the revelation of the composer's mind.

There has just reached me an interesting book by an American writer, Mr Pierre Key ('This Business of Singing'), in which we have an interesting light on Caruso's attitude towards this question of interpretation in opera. 'I keep my voices', he said to Mr Key, 'in a sort of drawer. When I am to sing Radames I take out of one drawer my Radames voice. It is heavy and dramatic in fibre. For Nemorino, in 'L'Elisir d'Amore', I turn to another drawer in that cabinet for a lighter quality of voice. And during the day when I have a performance I try to keep in the mood of the character I am to sing that evening, so that my voice as well as my thoughts will be in keeping with what I am to do on the stage. An artist does not sing Vasco di Gama's music in 'L'Africana' with the same weight of tone he uses for that of Lionel in 'Marta'. He approaches a song that is not operatic with consideration of the style demanded; and he suits his tones to fit. To adopt one weight and general colour of voice for every piece of music is to be mechanical, inartistic, and vocally limited.'

There are very few opera singers, however, who are such perfect singers as Caruso was; and even Caruso's precepts do not cover the whole ground. His triumphs were in Italian and French opera; and it is no disparagement of these genres to say that in general they do not confront the singer with anything like the same psychological difficulties as the Wagner operas. We have had many excellent Des Grieux, and Manricos, and 'Rigoletto' Dukes, and Fausts, and Romeos, and Rodolfos; but who, in this generation, has seen a single Siegfried or Brynhilde that he could persuade himself was the whole character as Wagner conceived it?

A great operatic character, in fact, calls for so many qualities in the singer that it is not to be wondered at that in ninety-nine cases out of a hundred the thoughtful spectator leaves the theatre, at best, only half satisfied. We may get, as with Flagstad, good singing, and for that we are very grateful: but Flagstad's Isolde or Brynhilde is not psychologically on the level of Wagner's. On the other hand, when we do get an actor who can make us really live in a part, the chances are that he has not the voice for it. We had an illustration of this in the performance last year of 'Tristan' by the Dresden opera company. The Tristan on that occasion, Julius Pölzer, had no voice to speak of; yet many of us thought him, on the whole, the best Tristan we have ever seen, especially in the third act. People who listen to opera simply for singing's sake, on the other hand, could get no pleasure at all out of his performance.

Argument about the matter is quite useless; the difference of opinion about it comes from a fundamental difference in the various listeners' point of view. It is not that those of us who found Pölzer's performance so engrossing are insensitive to beautiful singing; it is simply that an opera like 'Tristan' is a complex affair, and no amount of good singing in the abstract will compensate us for a reading of the part of Tristan that never succeeds in placing before us the mind of the character as Wagner conceived it. The ideal thing, of course, would be an impersonation like Pölzer's plus perfect singing. But that is an impossibility, the operatic world being what it is. In actual experience we have to put up with one of two things—reasonably good singing but no Tristan in the full sense of the word, or the real Tristan with dubious singing. What I found myself doing that evening, after I had got over my first feeling of disappointment with Pölzer as a singer, was to close down my critical faculties in this one field and concentrate on the fine intellectual qualities of the performance; and, as I have said, I came away with the feeling that for once I had seen Wagner's Tristan as he really is.

All this does not mean that people of my way of thinking do not mind what kind of singing they get in opera so long as the actor knows the inner meaning of what he is saying and singing. It all depends on the circumstances of the moment: just as no amount of good singing could satisfy me if the central conception of the character were faulty, so no amount of good acting could satisfy me if the singing were really bad. Pölzer's singing was not bad in the sense that it was offensive to the physical ear: it was simply that it was not 'singing' in the full sense of that term. I imagine that he is not a born singer, but a highly intelligent man who has made, by hard work, some sort of voice for himself in order that he may have some sort of a medium through which to realise his extremely subtle conception of a great work.

Coleridge has told us that we accept the Ghost scenes in 'Hamlet' not because we believe in ghosts, but because for the moment, for the purposes of the drama, we suspend our disbelief in ghosts. In much the same way I did not believe, when listening to Pölzer's Tristan, that this, in the abstract, was good singing, but I temporarily suspended my general disbelief in some at any rate of the disabilities attaching to imperfect singing. I could probably not have sat out a performance of Tristan in which I had been given merely Pölzer's voice without

Pölzer's brains. But as it was, I found it easy, after the first ten minutes or so, to make all the necessary allowances—to ignore the actual tones and concentrate on the fineness of the mentality at the back of this reading of Tristan. I still feel today that of all the Continental tenors I have heard in the part in recent years, Pölzer is the only one who would draw me to a theatre in anything but a professional capacity.

Opera, in fact, is a complex of so many things that we cannot reasonably expect every factor in a performance to be anything like perfect. Listening to even the best opera performance is a matter of tolerating this or that in consideration of being given something else that is worth having for its own sake. But one thing is certain—that good 'singing' in the common acceptation of that term is not of itself enough in opera. The intelligent spectator, who knows the work he is listening to and has done a good deal of thinking of his own about it, is not to be fobbed off with mere 'singing' if everything else that makes the opera what it was for the creator of it is lacking.

THIS BUSINESS OF SINGING:

CAN SCIENCE HELP?

S<small>IR</small> M<small>ILSOM</small> R<small>EES</small> seems to have created a sensation with his recent address before a learned gathering in which he said that the vocal cords were not put into the human throat for the purpose of singing. Some of us, it is true, had long suspected this, less on scientific grounds than on the evidence of our agonised ears at the opera and elsewhere. Who, for instance, who has listened to a typical Alberich doing what Mr Creevey describes old Talleyrand doing in some London drawing-room or other—'making the cursedest nasty noises in his throat'— could possibly bring himself to believe that he was watching the operation of a really natural physiological function? Such journalistic comment as I saw on Sir Milsom Rees's dictum was not very impressive: apparently the naïve reaction of the plain man to that dictum was that the vocal cords must have been put there for singing, or how could people sing? I fancy, however, that a consideration so simple as all that must have occurred to Sir Milsom long ago, and that consequently if it did not weigh with him there can't be much in it. His thesis, I fancy, is just this—that the vocal cords *can* be made to do all that is demanded of them in singing, at any rate for a time, but that it goes against the grain with them to do some of these things; so that sooner or later they rebel, with the result either that the voice 'goes' or the singer has to keep his end up by a variety of fakes, some of them very clever, some of them not so clever; moreover, that the throat specialist has the most conclusive visible evidence of the physical damage inflicted upon the throat by the persistent effort of many singers to make the cords do more than they were ever intended by nature to do.

On the scientific side I think we may take Sir Milsom's word for it. He is an eminent authority not only on the throat in general but on the singing throat in particular: in his forty years' experience as laryngologist to Covent Garden he has examined the mechanism of practically every singer of distinction; he has made a special study of the connection between singing and singers' laryngeal troubles; and I think we may take it for granted that he knows what he is talking about. However, I am not going to argue the scientific question on my own account. For one thing, it would take me out ot my depth. For another, there are some fifty thousand teachers of singing in this country alone, each of them, on his own admission, being the sole possessor of the secret of perfect 'voice production'; and I know, from painful experience, that if I begin to discuss singing, at least forty-nine thousand eight hundred and ninety-six of these gentlemen will write to me on the subject. So if any of them should feel inclined to write to me about it, let me assure them here and now that I agree with everything they may have to say before they say it.

Few will deny, I suppose, that the standard of singing is lower now than it has been for something like two centuries. I am not referring to artistry in interpretation: that is another matter altogether, and one in which the present-day standard is remarkably high. I am dealing purely and simply with singing in the sense of the production of exceptionally beautiful tone: and in that sense, I take it, everyone will agree that the day of the great voices is about over. A voice so fine that it attracts world-wide attention simply as a musical instrument is so rare a product that in any one decade nature seems incapable of throwing out more than about six or eight out of all earth's millions. Various readers may feel inclined to alter or add to the following lists according to their personal fancy: but, broadly speaking, each of them, I think, sums up its epoch fairly.

Born between 1840 and 1850 were Patti, Maurel, Maas, Materna, the two Vogls, Lilli Lehmann, Pauline Lucca, and Christine Nilsson. In the next decade come Albani, Nordica, Litvinne, the two de Reszkes, Plançon, Tamagno, and Battistini. These were exceptional vintage years. After that, it seems to me, the ground tends to become less fruitful in respect either of quantity or of quality or of both. Between 1860 and 1870 were born Melba, Ternina, Gulbranson, Eames, and Nevada: between 1870 and 1880—quite a good decade this

—Caruso, Ackté, Destinn, Chaliapin, Van Rooy, Kirkby Lunn, and Clara Butt: between 1880 and 1890, Elena Gerhardt, Julia Culp, and Frieda Hempel. The singers born between 1890 and 1900 comprise virtually all those who are now active among us; and I ask the reader to decide for himself how many, if any, of these deserve to rank with the great names of the past. Let me once more remind him that the question before us is not of singers who command our respect for their qualities of musicianship, culture, and general intelligence, but purely and simply of *voices*, of the kind that arouse universal enthusiasm on their own account, whether or no—occasionally no— they happen to be reinforced by the other qualities I have mentioned.

It would almost seem as if nature concentrated cyclically on the production of fine voices: the years 1841-1845 (Patti, Nilsson, Lucca), 1850-55 (Jean and Edouard de Reszke, Plan-çon, Tamagno, Albani), 1861-1865 (Melba, Nevada, Eames, Gulbranson, Ternina), 1870-1873 (Van Rooy, Caruso, Chalia-pin, Lunn, Butt, the last four all being born in 1873) represent a special effort on her part. Why there should be these cycles of boom and slump I leave it to scientists, philosophers and mystics to determine if they can. It may, for all I know, have something to do with sun-spots, or perhaps the Message of the Great Pyramid.

Whether anything can be done scientifically in the matter would be an interesting subject for research and experiment. An easy solution of the problem would perhaps be to go back to seventeenth and eighteenth century methods of making male sopranos and contraltos. Our ancestors' testimony as to the superlative beauty and power and flexibility of these artificially manufactured voices can be accepted unhesitatingly: they were so greatly superior in every way to the ordinary tenor that this latter order of voice was held in poor esteem. However, it is improbable that we shall ever revert to the methods of our forefathers. Is any other method possible? Will science ever be able to produce the kind of voice it wants, and in the numbers it would like, by intelligent breeding? The question is not a new one; confident answers have even been given to it. I have long tried, but in vain, to obtain a book with the portentous title 'Mégalanthropogénésie', by one Robert, that seems to have been published in the early years of the nineteenth century. This Robert appears to have maintained that a child will inherit the genius of its father if it is conceived under conditions peculiarly associated with the exercise of that genius, 'ainsi le général, le veille d'une grande bataille, le poète composant, et même le danseur'. 'Je suis persuadé', said this scientist, 'que si Vestris [the greatest ballet dancer of his epoch] s'acquittait de ses devoirs conjugaux après le ballet de "Télémaque" ou de "Psyché", il ne pourrait manquer d'engendrer un fils digne de lui, surtout ayant epousé une nouvelle Terpsichore.' The British Association for the Advancement of Science might take up this idea and see what can be done of with it.

I am indebted for my information about this daring spirit Robert to Champfleury, who, in some notes in his 'Souvenirs et Portraits de Jeunesse' (1872), tells us also of 'another reformer, M. Bernard Moulin', who contended that 'les enfants sont, à l'état physique, moral et intellectuel, la photographie vivante de leurs parents générateurs, prise au moment de la conception.' M. Moulin is kind enough to give us the 'recipe for making one's child a musician'. It runs thus: 'Tous les maîtres de musique n'ont pas des rejetons musiciens; il en serait autrement s'ils voulaient, au moment décisif, fredonner avec attention une cantate qui agite les fibres. Nous leur prédisons un succès complet; car en chargeant ainsi le fluide vital reproducteur, l'organe musical se photographiera vivant et magique dans le rejeton . . . L'enfant naîtra musicien.'

That seems fairly easy; but there is just one little catch, which Champfleury expresses thus: 'Ce fredonnement, la première nuit des noces, aurait pour résultat d'étonner profondement une mariée qui ne serait pas au courant du système de son époux.' Still, the first steps in a new science are notoriously the most difficult; and until M. Moulin's system, or that of M. Robert, has been put to the test on a sufficiently large scale of experiment and proved to have broken down, I shall continue to believe that something could be done scientifically to transmit a singing father's or mother's talent to the offspring.

MORE ABOUT SINGING:

FROM HOMOGENEITY TO HETEROGENEITY

12th September 1937

THERE was one possible reply to my article of last week so obvious that I am not surprised to find that none of my correspondents has lighted upon it. I am therefore compelled to attempt it myself.

Before we begin to dogmatise about the present condition of singing, would it not be as well to make sure what we mean by the term? *Is* there such a thing as 'singing' *per se*? The musical vocabulary in general is painfully inadequate to express distinctions, the result being the grave misunderstanding that always arises when different people, or perhaps we ourselves, employ the same standardised term to describe quite different things. We speak of counterpoint, for instance, as if it meant quite definitely just one thing; whereas the truth is that Palestrina counterpoint and Bach counterpoint are two very different things, not merely in their procedure but in the habit of mind, the musical orientation, in which they respectively have their origin. Because of the poverty of our nomenclature, we apply the same term, 'symphony' to an early Haydn work, the Eroica, and the Sibelius No. 7, though the ultimate purpose, the inner world of which the music is the mirror, and the technical means adopted to make this particular piece of music the mirror of that particular world, are as different from each other as chalk from cheese. And, to extend the illustration, is it not clear that the old term 'singing' is inapplicable *en masse* to the various artistic activities we subsume under that term today?

If any branch of human activity could serve better than any other to elucidate the Spencerian formula of evolution as a constant widening out from the homogeneous to the heterogeneous, from the undifferentiated to the differentiated, it would be music. As early as the seventeenth century the theorists began to be conscious of a 'modern' splitting up of the species into types. As one writer of that epoch put it, 'music' for a long time had meant just one thing: composers used, for instance, precisely the same idiom and the same technique for sacred music and for secular, for the madrigal as for the mass; whereas in *his* more enlightened epoch, as the writer proudly points out, they had no less than three orders of music corresponding to three different ways of feeling about things— one style for church music, one for chamber music, and one for opera.

If Berardi could return to earth today he would perhaps be astonished at the extent to which this differentiation has proceeded in a further century and a half. New species have sprung up of which he never dreamed; while each of these has branched out into sub-species more remarkable for their differences than for their resemblances. 'Opera', for instance, can now mean things so unlike each other as 'Don Giovanni', 'Aïda', 'Tristan', and 'Pelléas and Mélisande'. We have only the one word, 'song', for things so unlike each other as the Lieder of Schubert, Brahms, Wolf, Mahler, and Fauré. And so long as we continue to use the same old term for fundamentally different things, so long will we continue to make the mistake of judging this sub-species or that by the laws that determine the being of another, to the vast confusion of our critical standards, such as they are.

Now singing meant for a long time, and until quite recently, something quite other than what it means today. Singing has become differentiated into species and sub-species, and only aesthetic muddle can result from applying the old generic term to all of these. The singing of the older type was a particular product spontaneously evolved to meet the requirements of a particular kind of music. That music, for a very long time, was virtually undifferentiated: it called for not only a standard ideal of tone and management of tone, but a standard style of expression. The physical and mental apparatus suitable to one opera or oratorio aria was applicable with the minimum of change to any other. This homogeneity of purpose and of the means by which that purpose could best be realised, has given way, under the stress of evolution, to a baffling heterogeneity. Subtleties of psychology have come into play of which the older composers and singers had no conception. Any tenor (or male soprano) who could sing one Handel operatic aria could sing another: any soprano who could sing Pamina's 'Ach, ich fühl's' could sing Susanna's 'Deh! vieni, non tardar', although the one aria is an expression of grief and the other an expression of the amorous. But today the tenor who is ideal for 'Celeste Aïda' is far from ideal for Tristan or Pelléas, and vice versa: while the soprano who can easily bring out all there is in one Wolf song cannot bring out a fraction of what there is in another of a completely different mental cast.

A new conception of what singing would have to mean was forced upon the world by Wagner for the simple reason that it was forced on himself by the very nature of his creations. He did not want his operas to be declaimed or barked. He wanted them to be sung; but the kind of singing he wanted hardly existed in his early and middle days. What he said, in effect, was this: 'Italian voice production and Italian methods of expression are admirable things in and by themselves. But they came by a natural process out of a certain kind of music and a certain kind of mentality; and therefore they are inapplicable to music like mine, which starts from a different point from the Italian and moves towards a different goal. My music is German music: my mind is a German mind: I must therefore have voices and style suitable to my music and to the characters I portray in it. I want German teachers to produce first-rate voices, but not to make the old mistake of modelling them on the Italian. For one thing, our German throats are not built like the Italian, and therefore cannot vocalise in the same way; for another, a highly consonantal language like the German cannot possibly be intoned in the same way as a mainly vowel language like the Italian; for another, the suggestions of Italian opera mentality that are inseparable from singing of the older international opera type are quite alien to purely German characters and German emotions.

'Every argument that can be put forward to prove the perfection of the Italian opera voice and style is an argument against the employment of them in operas that neither musically, linguistically, mentally, or racially have any congruence whatever with Italian opera. In every past epoch a particular style of composition has been organically allied with a particular style of performance. The action and interaction between the two have been perfect: composers have written for certain instruments knowing that those instruments were the ideal ones for their music, while conversely the very existence and easy applicability of these instruments has controlled the thinking of the composers. Well and good. But here is a new kind of art, that can be realised adequately only on a new kind of instrument. Since that instrument does not exist, we must make it.'

So far Wagner. But the line of evolution from the homogeneous to the heterogeneous has not stopped with him. The types of music, and the types of mind behind the music, have become more and more differentiated since his day; and we have only to develop his own principle still further to see that vocal instruments of more and more differentiated types are being called for almost each decade. In spite of the differences between the contemporary Bach and Handel, or between the contemporary Haydn and Mozart, it still remains true that their resemblances over-ride their differences, and that certain broad principles of performance are applicable to the music of each member of each pair. But in the present day the differences between contemporary composers are greater than their resemblances, and the human instruments or the methods of procedure that suit one to perfection hardly suit another at all.

The musical world pretty well agrees by now that a conductor who is admirable in one composer's music may be a failure in another's. Those of us who spend most of our time in concert rooms and opera houses know, to our cost, that singers are constantly attempting tasks for which they are not suited. The average recital programme, for instance, is beyond the capacity of any singer. The wise recitalist is he who knows his limitations and chooses songs that all lie well within them. The less wise recitalist, who attempts in the same evening a Bach aria, a Verdi or Ponchielli scena, a Purcell song, a succession of Schubert, Schumann, Brahms and Wolf Lieder that call for an infinity of vocal timbres, of styles, and of intellectual and emotional understanding, merely courts disaster.

The tendency, as I see it, is all towards further specialisation in this as in everything else. It is useless for a baritone, the secret of whose appeal is a moving natural elegiac quality in the voice, and an intense sympathy with certain defeatist human moods, to try to sing heroic parts; and vice versa. Our singers will have to go the way of our actors, especially of our film actors. The days when an actor could impose himself upon his audience tonight as Romeo, tomorrow as Figaro, the following night as Tartuffe, and so on, are gone, probably for ever. What happens now, broadly speaking, is that an actor is cast for the particular type of part which his features, his stature, his voice, his manner, his mannerisms, and so on especially qualify him, and for no other type to the end of his days. So it will more and more tend to become with the singer. Already we see, in Wagner opera, a few singers specialising in certain parts to the exclusion of all others. That process will soon have to be extended to the concert room. There will be no 'Wolf singers', for the simple reason that no singer on earth has all the varieties of vocal timbre, of style, of mental perception, required to cover every type of Wolf song. What we will get is Wolf singers of the passionate type, Wolf singers of the elegiac type, Wolf singers of the ironic type, and so on.

'Singing' of the older abstract type, in which all that was required was a fine voice and good taste in the traditional style, is virtually dead and done with, except in connection with the music that was explicitly written with a view to the exploitation of those qualities. A beautiful voice is no longer a passport to any and every kind of music; on the contrary, there may be something in the peculiar nature of the very beauty of the voice that completely unfits it for interpreting certain characters or moods. Some time ago I heard a baritone of considerable accomplishment within his own sphere singing Sachs's two songs from the 'Meistersinger'. They could not have been better *sung*; the voice was first-rate, the singer was a man of culture. Yet the total effect of it all was no more like Sachs than a sycamore is like an oak. Partly because of something in the very timbre of the voice, partly because of the many suggestions of a personal mentality and a cultural environment that had nothing in common with Wagner, everything that Wagner had in his mind when he wrote the words and the music was missed. Our audiences, in the main, are as yet not very sensitive to discrepancies and anomalies of this kind in singing. But they will become increasingly conscious of them; and the time is bound to come when singers will see the wisdom of not attempting to cover more of the vast field of music than their natural limitations lay open to them.

PITY THE POOR BASS

15th April 1945

I RECEIVED the other day a letter that almost broke my too tender heart. It was from the possessor of a genuine bass voice well known to radio listeners. He complained of the shabby treatment that voices of his compass have had from the song composers; 'why', he asks, 'did the great Lieder writers set such an overwhelming majority of their songs for the high voice?' A statistical examination of their works has led him to the following conclusions:

'Schubert: speaking from memory, all the cycles and 70 or 80 per cent of his other songs are in high keys. Schumann: Pretty much the same. Brahms: in three albums (Peters edition) containing 164 songs, only 32 originally written in low keys. Wolf: a typical example—39 songs in the first three Mörike volumes with only three in low keys. I think we shall find a similar proportion in other Lieder writers. Of course I know there are outstanding exceptions, like the Brahms Ernste Gesänge, the Wolf Harfenspieler, etc., but they are few and far between.

'In fact, I should say that the genuine bass songs in the whole German repertory would not provide more than two or three recitals. I can find no satisfactory reason for this prevailing prejudice against singers with deep voices. . . . It has been suggested that these composers thought in keys and left the voice to take care of itself; but surely in that case, according to the law of averages, the result should be about fifty-fifty? The preference for high keys is too persistent and universal to be the outcome of mere chance.'

Here is a grave problem indeed. Perhaps my correspondent's figures are not wholly accurate: in the first 39 of the Mörike songs, for instance, I find not three but five songs in the bass compass; and of course there are several out-and-out bass songs, in particular the three Michelangelo Lieder, in Wolf's later works. Then again there are many songs written in the treble clef that might lead the casual observer to think they were intended for a tenor, whereas they lie well within the bass compass—Schubert's 'Prometheus', for instance, which ranges between the high E natural and the low B natural. Still, my correspondent seems to be right in his general contention.

A swift survey of German Lieder which I have made indicates, however, that many a fine song, bass in mentality, is barred to the true bass merely because of one or two high notes in climaxes. This phenomenon is interesting because we have on record a notable case of what was really intended for an operatic bass rôle having become the property, for the most part, of the bass-baritones, because of a few upper notes that are beyond the true bass compass. The case is that of Wotan, and it is particularly interesting just now because in the present dearth of first-rate deep voices the rôle is being undertaken in at least one foreign opera house not even by a bass-baritone but by a baritone. But we have Wagner's express statement, in one of his letters, that for his Wotan he had had in mind a pure bass, and that to obtain this ideal he would have no objection to the occasional high notes being replaced by lower ones.

There seems to be something, then, in my correspondent's suggestion that composers are inclined just to 'think in keys and leave the voice to take care of itself'. I myself would put it in a slightly different way: it is probable that in many cases they have had in mind a sort of generalised 'high voice' or 'low voice', but either because they have only the vaguest idea of vocal technique or because, lost in the fine frenzy of inspiration, they have lost touch with practicalities, they have been unaware that at one point and another they have shifted over from one voice-type to another. Debussy's Pelléas is ostensibly a tenor, but in practice the part is not ideal for any type of voice; Debussy, when writing the music, was thinking in terms of his own voice, which was of no recognised species.

Brahms, again, describes his Four Serious Songs as for 'bass voice'; and certainly if any songs are pure bass in their mentality it is these. Yet a pure bass is not comfortable with the occasional high F's and F sharps and with the climactic G of the last song; it is not so much a matter of simply 'getting' the notes as of keeping phrase and colour and atmosphere intact in so high a tessitura. Consequently we find a deep bass like Kipnis transposing the second song down half a tone and the other three down a full tone in the records made for the H.M.V. Brahms Society; and rightly so, for the gravity of the pure bass timbre in the songs as a whole is far more important than the precise pitch of three or four exceptional high notes.

We will continue with the subject next week, when I shall have something to say which, I hope, will bring solace to the wounded heart of my bass correspondent.

CONSOLATION FOR THE BASSES

22nd April 1945

I GAVE last week one or two reasons for not agreeing that the composers in general have been as 'prejudiced' against the bass as my correspondent tried to make out. Perhaps another answer to the question 'Why do they write a larger proportion of their Lieder for high voice?' would be that composers for the most part take only a narrow conventional view of the vast field of poetry. They appear to imagine that the thing most suitable for singing about is love, successful, disastrous, or merely speculative; and for that trite theme the tenor, for some occult reason or other, is generally regarded as nature's own medium. But when the composers get on to loftier subjects, such as *haute politique*, conspiracy, wine-bibbing, the damnation of souls, or murder of the finer kind, then far more often than not it is to the low voice that they instinctively turn.

The plain proof of this is afforded by their practice in opera and oratorio. Here the composer is not only free to cater for the low as well as the high voices but he must do so; and we have only to run an eye over the repertory to see that for his more intelligent characters he prefers the lower voice to the higher. (I rule out Wagner, who, being in the habit of doing not only his musical but his dramatic thinking for himself, endowed, perhaps over-optimistically, even his tenor characters with brains.)

To establish this broad proposition I shall lump basses and bass-baritones and baritones together. The 'hero' parts are mostly stereotyped: the 'hero' of most stories is, by convention, in love with some chit or other, and so the composer blindly follows convention a step further and makes him a tenor. Brains are not, strictly speaking, a necessary part of his equipment; Radames, for instance, owed his appointment as Commander in Chief of the Egyptian land forces not to any military genius but simply and solely to the fact that he was the only man in Egypt with a B flat *in alt*. Certain tenor parts of course, have been quite rightly cast for that type of voice—

rôles in which inexperienced beardless youth and a certain mental innocence are of the essence of the character; we could hardly imagine a bass Tamino, Des Grieux, Pelléas, Romeo or Ottavio.

But nearly all the roles that imply the possession of an intelligence and a character, good or bad but anyhow a bit out of the common, are allotted to the lower male voices. Further, most of the companionable people, the likeable rascals, the jolly topers, the artful dodgers, are basses or baritones. Just look at a few of the names on the honourable list: Sarastro, Mephistopheles, Pizarro, Don Giovanni, Figaro, Cornelius's Barber, Wotan, Hagen, Iago, Scarpia, Boris, Prince Igor, Khan Kontchak, Ivan the Terrible, the Muleteer in 'L'Heure Espagnole', Tchaikovsky's Mazeppa, Mozart's Don Alfonso, Baron Ochs, Falstaff, Don Pasquale, Osmin, Eugen Onegin, Varlaam, Gianni Schicchi, Amfortas, Handel's Polyphemus, Gounod's Vulcan, Sullivan's Friar Tuck; and so ad infinitum.

The tenors are fobbed off with the ranting parts, the puling parts, the self-pitying parts, the easy amorous parts, the intellectually naive parts: the basses and baritones get the best thinking parts, the best drinking parts, the scheming and the doing parts: they get the kings and the statesmen and the high priests and the fiends and the philosophers and the better class of assassin.

I put it squarely to any man of ordinary intelligence— would you choose Faust and Romeo and Cavaradossi and Dmitri and Ottavio and Fenton and Rinuccio and Samson for an evening's company (or, for that matter, Mélisande and Marguerite and Gilda and Juliet and Michaëla); when you could talk and clink glasses with men and women of the world like Mephistopheles and Scarpia and Boris and Don Giovanni and Falstaff and Gianni Schicci and Maddalena and Carmen and Delilah? No; it is evident enough that these low-voice characters are the ones the composer has loved most, for he has generally given them his most original music. So the low-voice singers can take heart; if the Lieder writers, slaves to convention, have too often fallen sobbing at the feet of the tenors and sopranos, the opera composers, men with a broader outlook on life, have proved conclusively that they prefer the basses, baritones and contraltos.

THE NON-MUSICAL PRODUCER

20th June 1948

IT is no part of my purpose, even if it were within my competence, to teach producers, purely as such, their jobs. Production, like all other highly specialised activities, should be left to the specialist, for whom alone, in matters of art, I have any respect. Where, however, as in musical drama, the field of operation is a composite of territories subject to different artistic jurisdictions, the critical spectators may legitimately suggest that a procedure that may be fully valid in one of these may be invalid, or even fatal, in another. It is more especially the non-musical producer of opera who needs an occasional friendly reminder from musicians of this fundamental fact.

My main contention is that since music is the most potent of all the factors in musical drama, the producer who cannot mentally re-live an opera in terms of music, but works upon the libretto just as he would upon the text of a spoken play, cannot possibly convey to the spectator, because he himself cannot possibly realise it, what the work is really 'about'.

A little while ago I was told of a young enthusiast who had just heard 'Tristan' for the first time and had been shocked by the immobility of Tristan and Isolde during their long colloquy in the second act. Surely, he said, they could be given something to 'do' to keep the thing 'moving'. That young man should watch his step; if he isn't careful he may grow up to be one of those producers who can conceive opera only in terms of the ordinary stage.

The drama of 'Tristan' is for the most part static. Hardly anything 'happens'; the drama is inside the two chief characters, the outcome of what they are and previously were in themselves, not of their reaction to this or that external event of the moment. The spectator, the singer, the conductor or the producer who is not aware of this basic fact, but shares the current fatuous notion that the long scene in the second act is just a 'love duet', has simply never got within a hundred miles

77

of the most elementary understanding of what 'Tristan and Isolde' is 'about'. These two are not ordinary 'lovers'; and to break in upon their physical quiescence with any of the transparent little stage dodges by which an appearance of 'movement' is given to a long scene in spoken drama is the last word in absurdity.

All through the second act, except near the end of it, when Wagner wants a dramatic climax, he obtains it by purely musical means which are beyond the understanding of the producer who is not himself acutely musical. A case in point is the moment when Isolde, resolved to bring Tristan to her, decides to extinguish the torch—the symbol of hateful Day: at the words 'The Queen of Love's will it is that Night shall come upon us and alone give us [inner] light' he conveys the sense of climax by a sudden great enlargement of the melodic line in voice and orchestra. The device is simplicity itself, but it is tremendous in its effect; the least instructed listener in the theatre feels instinctively that here the emotional tension has attained its maximum and must somehow find release. But the psychological point is essentially and profoundly a musical one; the non-musical producer will never discover it by himself.

'Tristan' is of course an exceptional case; but the general principle holds good for all serious opera. Music brings into the drama a super-potent element, that of an idealisation beyond the scope of words; and nothing should confront us on the stage that blurs this idealisation with touches of too crude reality. The music, needless to say, is not the entire drama; but there should be nothing in the visible action that is not in the 'key' of the music. It is because this rudimentary fact was overlooked by someone or other that the inn scene of 'Boris Godounov' will always remain in the memory of some of us as the most mistaken thing of its kind in all our operatic experience.

Opera, in fact, is *musical* drama, while spoken drama is just drama. Neither stage movement, however smartly true to life in the ordinary theatrical sense, nor scenic setting, however pretty as a picture, can save any opera production from being a bad production if the producer is not musical enough to be sensitive to the mental 'key' of the music as a whole and from moment to moment. For an instance of the ideal correspondence of the key, the 'feel' of the stage picture with that of the music, I would select the late Hugo Rumbold's exquisite design for 'L'Heure Espagnole' in one of the Covent Garden seasons of long ago. Even the degree and the very timbre of the lighting should play its subtle part in the total spiritual impression: I have yet to see in London a perfect correspondence between the light that floods the final scene of 'Fidelio' and the mighty C major of the music.

ACTING IN OPERA

I

I HAVE heard dramatic critics speak disrespectfully of the kind of acting they see when they pay a visit to the opera. But 'acting' has not the same meaning in opera as in spoken drama, the conditions of character-portrayal being entirely different in the two genres. Neither the starting-point nor the goal is the same.

The opera singer has to do his work under peculiar and hampering conditions. His primary preoccupation is bound to be with the technical business of singing well; and whereas speaking is a natural, everyday human function, singing is a more or less artificial one, involving certain inhibitions of the ordinary free play of the facial muscles.

A good actor of the part of Tamino, rapturously contemplating the portrait of Pamina and musing 'How wondrous beautiful this face' (a rough English equivalent of 'Dies Bildnis ist bezaubernd schön'), could grace the words with a dozen artful little inflections of tone and colour and rhythm, and illuminate them by a dozen little tricks of facial expression. But the singer of the words has to follow humbly a line traced out for him in every detail by the composer; on the second syllable, for instance, he has no choice but to immobilise his mouth for a time that would seem to the ordinary actor an eternity, since the note that Mozart has prescribed for this syllable is three times the length of each of the five that follow it in the bar.

Looking at the matter from another angle, it becomes evident that the positions imposed upon a singer's mouth by the production of a given musical sound may make it impossible for him to reinforce by facial expression the 'bite' of a word or a phrase. The reader can easily test this for himself. He will find it easy enough to elongate his mouth laterally to convey a particular nuance of the disagreeable if the words he is singing exploit the longitudinal 'e' ('screech', 'sneer', 'beast', etc.), but difficult or impossible if the librettist, having no experience or knowledge of singing, has expressed the mental state in question in words in which the rounded 'o' predominates.

The singer of such a line will find himself on the horns of a dilemma: the expression of the disagreeable image calls for a stretching of the lips, the shaping of the musical tone for a pursing of them. Chaliapine, it is true, could put his mouth into almost any position required by the 'acting' of the words and still produce an agreeable singing tone; but Chaliapines are rare.

Furthermore, as I have more than once pointed out, casting in opera goes more by larynxes than by physical build or presence. On the speaking stage a flyweight Agamemnon or a bantam Otello would be as unnecessary as ridiculous; but on the operatic stage the mere fact of the voice being tenor or bass, soprano or contralto, coloratura or noncoloratura, will determine the casting. Hence it comes about that we get Siegfrieds whose lack of inches has to be made up for by several all-too-visible thicknesses of boot-sole, and a Gilda, a Mimi, a Musetta, a Fidelio or a Salome of heaven knows how many tons displacement but who happens to have the right vocal range and volume for the music. To expect much 'acting' of the ordinary kind under conditions such as these is asking rather too much of poor humanity.

But there is another side to the matter, to which I will invite the reader's attention next week.

II

22nd July 1951

LAST Sunday I suggested that our friends the dramatic critics are a little hard on the acting of opera singers, and I pointed out one or two ways in which these worthy people are hampered by the very nature of the apparatus with which they have to work, particularly the fact that because they have to sing, not speak, they lack the opportunities for variety of facial expression enjoyed by the actor in a spoken play. This, however, is by no means the only handicap with which the opera singer has to contend.

The dramatic critic is revolted or amused, according to the bias of his temperament and the extent of his charity, at the spectacle of an alleged Tristan or Don Ottavio or Radames confronting us with mouth wide agape for a whole minute or two stock-still except for an occasional stereotyped motion of the arms. (When an opera character raises one arm we are to understand that something or other has moved him deeply; when he raises both arms that means that his soul has been shaken to its foundations.)

But all this is not his fault, but that of the Demiurge who millions of years ago created this curious cosmos. He foresaw most of the things that would happen on earth and duly provided not only for them but also for the counterforces necessary to ensure the eternal running of the machine; having arranged, for example, for an advance in science that will enable A to blow B into a thousand pieces, he squares matters by giving B the idea for an explosive that will enable him to blow A into two thousand; and so ad infinitum. But one thing, apparently, the Demiurge failed to foresee—the invention of opera, or at any rate the fact that in this multiple form of art the singer would have to rely for most of his dramatic expression on arm movements, and a mere pair of arms is a niggardly equipment for such a job.

Whenever I turn over the pages of a book on Indian or some other oriental art and see some god or hero in swaggering possession of four or six arms I cannot help regretting that opera singers have not been constructed on similarly generous lines. Think of how many permutations and combinations even four arms would be capable! They would make all kinds of psychological subtleties and contrarieties possible—as it were a counterpoint of gesture.

Everyone knows the story of Gluck's correction of the hasty critic who objected that it was absurd to make Orestes sing 'Now calm possesses my heart again' to an agitated orchestral accompaniment. 'Orestes is lying', said Gluck in effect: 'he has been the murderer of his mother, and the orchestra is contradicting him.' Now if the first player of the part of Orestes had had an extra pair of arms there might have been no misunderstanding on the critic's part and no need for explanation on Gluck's: the cross-currents in the hero's soul would have been made perfectly clear by cross-rhythms of the arms. With such an equipment, again, Otello, by a convulsive movement of the north-east arm, might convey to us that he was revengefully bent on murdering Desdemona, while by a counterpoint in a contrary rhythm in the south-west arm he could convince us that he still had a soft spot in his heart for the poor girl and very much regretted having to be so tough with her.

Or take the case of Zerlina in doubt whether to yield or not to Don Giovanni's smooth suggestion that he shall be allowed to entertain her at his villa and show her his stamp collection. 'Vorrei e non vorrei', she stammers, 'mi trema un poco il cor ... mi fa pietà Masetto; presto non son più forte'; 'I want to go and I don't; my heart's all of a flutter. Yet surely I might let myself kick over the traces for once. Of course I'm sorry for Masetto; but all the same I don't think I can hold out much longer.' (I translate freely, following the line of the little minx's thought rather than the actual verbal shorthand Da Ponte has put into her mouth.)

Imagine the complex of emotions that could be conveyed here by four arms! And then, when the ramparts are down and the fortress is taken, partly by storm, partly through treachery within the gates, and she and Giovanni unite in a cry of 'Come on, come on, my hawk, my pigeon; let us make up for lost time' —again I translate psychologically rather than verbally— what shifting nuances of the eternal subject and counter-subject of the Ewig-weibliche and the Ewig-männliche could be expressed by a sort of eight-part Bachian counterpoint of arms! But alas, opera singers, like the rest of us, are restricted to two.

It will not have escaped the reader's observation that the best operatic acting is generally given us by the minor characters, and particularly the comic ones; we have all seen some very good Leporellos and Mimes and Papagenos and Beck-messers, but hardly ever a really credible Tristan or Don Ottavio or Siegfried or Tamino. Into this matter I will go more closely next week, and at the same time try to show that even on the serious side opera has some cards up its sleeve that are denied to the actor in the spoken drama.

THE ORCHESTRA AS ACTOR

29th July 1951

To any opera singer who should ask me what he can do to improve his acting I would reply with a counter-question—Is your 'acting', as you call it by false analogy with the spoken drama, really necessary? For the factor that chiefly differentiates opera from ordinary drama—the music, and especially the orchestra—can make 'acting' supererogatory, for there the singer has a partner that as often as not takes the whole burden off his shoulders. I could cite numberless instances to illustrate this, but here I must confine myself to one in which the ordinary opera-goer will be able to follow me without any difficulty.

In the first scene of the third act of the 'Meistersinger' the young poet-knight is prevailed upon by Sachs to tell him his dream of the morning hours of the night before. This he does in what is commonly, though erroneously, spoken of as the Prize Song. The poem and the music, it is true, develop into the Prize Song in the final scene; but at the moment they are simply what our German friends, taking advantage of the licence of their language to create portmanteau words, succinctly call the 'Morgentraumdeutweise'—as we would say, 'the strain (words and music) that interprets the inner meaning of the morning dream'.

Now there is no need for the player of the part to do anything at all in the way of acting here, for everything that the best actor could do is done infinitely better by the orchestra. All the singer need do is in the first place to sing as he should (about this I shall have something to say later), and in the second place to follow the composer's plain directions how to suggest the attempt to recall the blissful morning dream. He is to 'compose himself', and then 'begin his song very softly, as if communing with himself.' That is all; everything else that is to establish the dream atmosphere is done in the orchestra.

The reader will remember that after Walther has decided to comply with Sachs's request there come four preludial bars for the orchestra alone. They begin with a softly-breathed chord in the lower strings, through which a harp arpeggio slowly ascends—as it were the dispersion of the morning mental mist. Then comes a quick crescendo; the chord is held for a while at its maximum, then slowly subsides into a long-drawn pianissimo. This volume-pattern, as we may call it, of the first two bars is repeated in the remaining two. For the full understanding of the procedure we have to go to the orchestral score, for the piano scores, so far as my knowledge of these extends, obscure or pervert the important basic facts.

The soft chord with which the tiny prelude ends is, like its predecessor at half-way, to be 'held for a long time' before it dies away; and so much importance did Wagner attach to the 'sehr lange' he has written over the stave that he added a further most explicit direction at the foot of the orchestral score: 'the two *fermate* must be of exceptionally long duration, and the ebb of tone after the swift upsurge of it must be very gradual.'

This four-bar prelude, then, paints to perfection the effort of the young poet to 'compose himself by self-communion', to recapture the dream state and objectivate it for Sachs (and us) in words and tones. And when the singer begins, Wagner accompanies him only with the muted strings at their softest and most veiled; it is as if the dream were only slowly bridging the gulf in the young man's mind between the subconscious and the conscious. I lack the space to describe in detail the gradual intensifications of orchestral colour as the long episode develops, the atmosphere changes, and the knight slowly passes from the hesitant effort to recapture the other-world dream to full this-world possession of it and realisation of its significance.

Wagner has thus provided in his scoring of the scene all that is required to make it psychologically clear to us. The singer has virtually no need whatever to 'act'; all he has to do is to sing in tone-colours and tone-volumes that shall be consubstantial with those of the orchestra. But this is precisely what the wretched man, as a rule, cannot do, for the simple reason that he cannot *sing* in the full sense of the term.

He begins conscientiously enough with an attempt at the 'piano, dolce' prescribed for the orchestra; but no sooner (after half a dozen bars or so) does the melody soar to the upper range of his voice than he bursts into a blaring fortissimo; for owing to the defects in his technique he finds it difficult to produce any other kind of tone at a high pitch. He ruins the episode for the intelligent listener, takes all the psychology, all the poetry out of it, not because he can't act but because, to put it bluntly, he can't sing. And in countless other cases in his repertory he sins against the light in the same crude way.

It is not to a school for acting that he needs to go but a school for singing. But this raises a new question: where in the world is the sort of school he and his like are so obviously in need of? It would have to be a school that paid quite as much attention to the singer's brain as to his larynx.

A NEW PATH?

30th March 1952

I ENDED my article last week with the query whether 'melo-drama' might not point the way to a possible escape from one dilemma of modern opera.

There are only four ways of running words and music in harness together.

(1) The words can be sung, they and the music combining to make an organic whole.

This means, in practice, that musical expression and musical form become the governing factors. When the desire arises, as it has done periodically in musical history, to allow words a much wider range, three modes of doing so present themselves:

(2) simple recitation of a long poem to illustrative music;

(3) a factitious compromise between speech and song, as in Schönberg;

(4) speech pure and simple in conjunction with music, as (in its simplest form) in the dungeon scene in 'Fidelio'.

Experience has proved that No. 2 raises more problems than it solves. For one thing, it is a pure impossibility to listen simultaneously to music-in-its-own-right and poetry-in-its-own-right: in practice the music generally asserts its own despotic claim, the poetry becoming merely devitalised prose.

To these theoretical difficulties others are added in perfor-mance. The speaking part is given as a rule to an actor, because of his training in rhetorical devices; and I have yet to meet with an actor who can speak poetry as people with a true poetic sense read it to themselves. Naturally, also, the speaker exaggerates his own importance in the joint undertaking. He *acts*, and over-acts, the words; and, not being a musician himself, and feeling that whatever else may be going on around him *he* must at all costs be heard and admired; he orates so loudly as to obscure much of the texture of the music. The result is that after one disagreeable experience of this sort no one feels an irresistible urge to ask for another; and so, to cite a concrete case, we practically never hear Schumann's 'Manfred', which contains much of his very finest music.

With No. 3 the musical world stubbornly refuses to have any truck. If the reciter in 'Pierrot Lunaire', for example, is an actress (not a singer), her points of contact with the musical element incarnated in the score are few and dubious. If she is a singer, her attempts to *speak* (not sing) at just-off the definite pitches indicated by the pseudo-melodic notes of the score become at times downright tragi-comic. The impulse to *sing* is so fundamental in her that while conscientiously trying to sheer away from the definite pitch she involuntarily keeps slipping on to it: then, realising suddenly that this isn't playing the game according to the rules laid down by the composer, she hastily slithers off it again. And, worst of all, our attempt to follow and enjoy the instrumental score in all its ingeniosities is frustrated by the annoyance set up in us by these unrelated vocal sounds that are always throwing the purely musical structure out of true, as it were.

I have often pleaded for a performance of 'Pierrot Lunaire' in which the words shall be simply read out before each section —so as to let the hearer have an idea of what it is all about— the instrumental part being allowed to stand by itself and speak for itself. Will not the B.B.C. give us just one experimental performance of this sort?

There remains, then, our No. 4, plain conversational speaking now and then while the music carries on freely in its own way. It is the oddest of paradoxes that this combination of the two stark opposites, music and speech, can be not only inoffensive in itself but made a telling dramatic infix in a texture otherwise given up wholly to music. A case in point is the colloquy in ordinary speech between Hoffmann, Niklaus, Schlemil and Dapertutto towards the end of the second act of 'The Tales of Hoffmann', while the orchestra sings softly and ironically the emotion-charged barcarolle. The dramatic tension is not dissipated, as we might have expected, by the sudden intrusion of speech into the domain of music, but positively and astonishingly enhanced by it.

88

Another case is Tosca's comment over the corpse of Scarpia—'And before this man all Rome trembled!' Puccini has designedly written the notes as a sombre monotone on the low C sharp of the soprano voice, the effect being practically that of simple speech.

We are surely entitled to ask, then, whether more systematic use cannot be made of this method of a dramatic grafting of speech *per se* upon the musical tissue of an opera. It will mean, of course, a new technique of libretto writing, but that would come with practice. Anyhow the experiment is worth trying: a new libretto technique is obviously one of the things opera is most in need of today.

PART III

COMPOSERS AND THEIR WORKS

HOLST'S CHORAL SYMPHONY

I

11th October 1925

Holst calls his new work, that was produced at the Leeds Festival on Wednesday, a 'First Choral Symphony', from which one gathers that he has sufficient faith in the vitality of the form to contemplate further adventures in it. This first essay is certainly tentative here and there, but on the whole the genre justifies itself. Whether it could do so indefinitely I should not like to say; it would depend largely, no doubt, not only on the composer but on good taste and good luck in the choice of poems.

The purist may, with fair reason, object to the title of 'symphony' being given to works of this class, for there is little analogy with the orchestral symphony beyond the fact that the new work is in four sections, corresponding superficially to the (a) Introduction and Allegro, (b) Adagio, (c) Scherzo, (d) Finale. Titles apart, the 'choral symphony' is just a setting of four poems (or extracts from poems) for chorus and a solo voice, with orchestral accompaniment. The form, whether new or old, is of no importance, and the nomenclature of less; all that matters is the quality of Holst's music.

London will have an opportunity of hearing the work in a couple of weeks or so, when the Leeds Choir will come here to sing it at the first Philharmonic concert. There will be a chance then, perhaps, to discuss the music in closer detail; here I propose to deal only with some general aesthetic aspects of the work.

The text is taken wholly from Keats—the Prelude, Song and Bacchanal (the first movement of the symphony) from 'Endymion', (the Invocation to Pan and the Roundelay, 'Beneath my palm trees, by the river side'), the Scherzo from 'Ever let the fancy roam' and the 'Folly's Song', the Finale from the 'Spirit Song', the 'Hymn to Apollo' and the 'Ode to Apollo';

in the slow movement the 'Ode on a Grecian Urn' is set entire. Holst's is the most restlessly enquiring and adventuring mind in the English music of today. He is experimenting simultaneously in three fields—that of harmony, that of rhythm in itself, and that of musical rhythm in a new synthesis with poetic rhythm. There is nothing 'experimental' about Holst, of course, in the disparaging sense in which that word is generally applied to some of the wilder musical adventures of today. Holst knows perfectly well what he is doing in every bar; his irregular rhythms move in complete freedom; the harmonies that look curious on paper are logical enough to the ear; and his way of setting words to music is at bottom only a reversion, at long last, to the fundamental principles of English musical prosody that were well understood by the Tudor composers. It is to this last point that I want to devote the remainder of my first article.

Vocal music everywhere is at last emancipating itself from the tyranny of the classical instrumental forms, with their fondness for short and symmetrical rhythmic phrases, and from the sing-song rhythms of the German Lied. The simple rhythms of the ordinary German poem, which remained unchanged, broadly speaking, from the time of Walther von der Vogelweid until recently, invited a corresponding rhythmic simplicity in the musical setting. When Germany took the lead in music, the vocal and the instrumental impulse flowed into the same channel and obeyed the same laws: the type of phrase that did well as a symphonic 'subject'—short, melodically clear-cut and expressive, and rhythmically definite—did equally well for the ordinary German song. In practically every other country also the vocal line took on much of the character of the instrumental, because of the strong unconscious 'pull' of the instrumentally developed sense of design; and after the great achievements of romantic German song had been added to those of German instrumental music, the tendency everywhere became more pronounced, on the part of vocal writers, to think in terms of musical metrics rather than in terms of poetic rhythm. In a fine Tudor song the longs and shorts of the melody, its accents, its caesura, its length of phrase, are largely determined by the corresponding elements in the verse; in later and modern times the tendency has been to submerge all the subtler rhythmical qualities of the verse under an evenly moving melodic flood, in which every wave is of the same length, and in which crest and trough, strong accent and weak, come at virtually corresponding distances each time.

Against this instrumental handling of words there came a revolt, partly conscious, partly unconscious, in the 19th century. It took different forms at different times in different countries. In Russia, Dargomijski, and after him Moussorgsky, tried to translate speech realistically into music, to turn the melodic line into a sort of recitative, in which the time values and the accents of the spoken line were reproduced as accurately as the nature of music and of singing would allow. These Russians failed, for the most part, because they misunderstood the nature of the problem. They saw it only as an affair of realism—of copying nature, as they put it. That is always the point of view of the amateur in music; and in spite of his genius there was a good deal of the amateur even in Moussorgsky. Neither he nor Dargomijski saw that the problem, though, sure enough, it was secondarily one of realism, was primarily one of music. If the musical ear is to be addressed and appealed to, it must be in terms of music *qua* music, not of music as an imitation of nature. To write an indeterminate vocal line that shall stress just the accents that would be stressed in speaking the words, and go up or down in just the same places and as near as possible to the same extent as the speaking voice would under similar circumstances, is not at all a difficult thing to do. Such realistic settings of the words as we have, for instance, in Moussorgsky's Children's Songs are within the powers of a thousand composers for every one who would find it within his powers to write the 'Mushrooms' or the 'Hopak'. The genre came to nothing: Moussorgsky wrote a whole opera in it ('The Matchmaker'), which he himself seems to have thought an improvement on 'Boris Godounov.' Posterity does not agree with him; the genre is too essentially non-musical to get much hold upon the musical listener.

In many parts of 'Pelléas and Mélisande' Debussy subordinated himself, as musician, to the poet, being content just

95

to speak the words to music. To many of us, these are now the weakest portions of the opera; they seem to us to evade, not solve, the problem, and to be so easy as hardly to be worth while. Operatic composers in general have not shown, since 'Pelléas and Mélisande', any desire to adopt the genre; it involves too complete a surrender of the composer's right as a musician.

Hugo Wolf attacked the problem in another way, and solved it. He gave back to the poet most of the rights that had been filched from him, but did not encroach upon the composer's rights in order to do so; he did not, like Moussorgsky, and Debussy in his weaker passages, rob the musician Peter to pay the poet Paul. On the contrary, he gave the musician a liberty he had not hitherto possessed in the song. Rhymes, of course, had to go, except when they coincided with a definite verbal period: no modern song composer pays, or can pay, much attention to these. But so far as the rest of the poem was concerned, Wolf treated the poet with a new respect. He did not, as Schubert sometimes did, throw the musical accent on to the wrong word to suit the exigencies of his melody, or treat the poetic line merely as a pretext for a beautiful quasi-instrumental phrase. He let the words roll out of the singer's mouth with the same accents, the same high and low lights, the same punctuation, the same length of sentence, as if they were being spoken. But being a great musician, with a technique far beyond Moussorgsky's, he had no need to sacrifice the music on the altar of the poetry. He saw that the problem was primarily one of counterpoint: the voice part had to follow the laws of free melodic declamation, the accompaniment had to develop independently along purely musical lines, and the two had to be welded together into an indivisible unity. No matter how autonomous the two may be, especially rhythmically, they must go together, and in the process of going together they must make music. It took a great technique, combined with a marvellous imagination, to do this.

Holst has approached the problem from yet another direction. I shall discuss his method of handling English poetry in another article.

II

18th October 1925

MILTON praised Henry Lawes for being the first (which he certainly was not) who

> . . . taught our English music how to span
> Words with just note and accent, not to scan
> With Midas' ears, committing short and long.

The historians, from Burney and Hawkins to Dr Ernest Walker, have dealt rather severely with Lawes and the claims made for him by his contemporaries. The trouble was that Lawes was not a good enough composer to make his generally careful scansion matter very much; it is not much use giving syllables their right accentual values if the melodic line is deficient in musical values. The eighteenth century, as typified in Burney and Hawkins, was hardly fitted to see the question in the round, for, as Hawkins's remarks in particular show, the smooth symmetrical Italian opera form of melody had taken such possession of men's minds that they were puzzled and irritated by any vocal line the even flow of which was broken every now and then to give this syllable or the other its verbal due. Hawkins described Lawes's music as being 'neither recitative nor air, but in so precise a medium [i.e. middle point] between both that a name is wanting for it'; 'the great and almost only excellence' of his songs is 'the exact correspondence between the accent of the music and the quantities of the verse.'

Just accentuation of itself will not redeem otherwise poor music; and nothing is gained by drawing attention, as Hubert Parry sometimes did in his songs, to the words by a niggling nicety of accent and quantity where it does not matter in the least,—ostentatiously writing such a word as 'weather', for example, as a quaver followed by a dotted crotchet to show that the composer knows, and wants us to know he knows, that the first syllable of the word should have stress but not duration.

The problem of setting English verse to music is much more complicated than this. It is possible, of course, to transgress against the poet and still make lovely and immortal music;

97

who is going to turn his back on 'Wie bist du, meine Königin' because of the wrongful pause in the melody at the end of the poet's first line, the sense of which is not completed till the second? But when all is said, it remains true that people with a feeling for poetry as well as for music will always desire a perfect fitting of the two in point of accent, phrase length, and so on. Of late years both the English and the German composers have given a great deal of attention to the subject; and in England no one has explored it more thoroughly and success- fully than Holst, who has the good luck to be an excellent composer as well as a sensitive poetic rhythmist.

It is not the least of his virtues that he is not the slave of any rigid scheme; he gets some of his finest effects in irregular measures, but if the effect can be got equally well in a regular measure he does not hesitate to use it. In the 'Choral Sym- phony' he often employs a seven-eight measure that has the advantage of allowing the singer to stress musically the weighty syllable of a line (or part of a line), and at the same time keep it as near speech as it is to music, by depriving the stress-note of the extra and superfluous time-value it would have in the usual setting. Take, for instance, Keats's lines:

> The earnest trumpet spake, and silver thrills
> From kissing cymbals made a merry din.

That even Holst can sometimes be led astray by a metric scheme is shown by the too great value he allows to the first syllable of 'kissing'; the first high light in that line should be the 'cym' of 'cymbals'. Errors of this kind, however, are rare with him. The strong caesura after 'spake' in the first line gets its full musical value in the musical phrase; the second line, that has no caesura, would have been rightly carried on but for the unfortunate stressing of 'kiss-', in one long phrase, with the high lights delicately touched in on 'cym-' and 'mer-'. The advantages of the seven-eight scheme may be seen in this example; 'trumpet' gets precisely its right verbal values, which it would not have had if the notes had been either two quavers (three-four time) or a dotted crotchet and quaver (four-four time); the voice poses itself just as long as is necessary on the 'trump-', and not a fraction of a second more.

The point is illustrated again in the following:—

which would have been set by an older school of composers thus:

This older school would have set another line thus:

whereas Holst gets it exactly right in this way:

The score of the 'Choral Symphony' teems with similar felicities. When variety is necessary, Holst's instinct supplies it. The line 'The earnest trumpet spake, and silver thrills' is paralleled precisely, so far as syllables, stresses, quantities and caesura are concerned, in the line 'Ah, happy, happy boughs, that cannot shed'. In his setting of the latter Holst abandons the seven-eight scheme for the normal eight-eight—

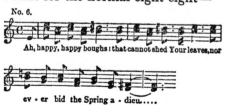

99

The justification of the change is to be found in the tempo. 'The earnest trumpet' line is sung in quick time; the pace is about that of the speaking voice, and a peculiar pleasure is given us by the musical phrase slipping off the tongue virtually as the spoken phrase would do. The 'Ah, happy boughs' is part of the adagio movement of the symphony. The slow tempo and the nature of the harmonisation predispose us to listen with relatively more of our musical and less of our poetic sense than in the former case, and the pausing of the voices on 'boughs' and 'leaves' for a fraction longer than they had previously done on 'trump'- and 'sil-' gives us a musical delight that we should have been unwilling to sacrifice for strict verbal metrics. Even here, however, Holst shows his instinct for the right thing. The succeeding lines are—

> And happy melodist, unwearied,
> For ever piping songs for ever new.

To have kept the same phrasing inside the bars for this as for the two preceding lines would have meant false accents at certain places. Holst gets everything right by entering after the bar-line instead of before it—

so that the strong beats of the bar coincide once more with the strong beats of the words.

'FAÇADE'

2nd May 1926

Oɴ Tuesday evening all the intellect of Chelsea was gathered into one small room to hear 'Façade', which Mr Osbert Sitwell, in a preliminary speech that was rather too cross-grained to be quite the right thing on so festive an occasion, rightly described as an entertainment. And a jolly good entertainment it was in many ways, and we should have enjoyed it still more had we been able to sit on cushions, in the daring, Bohemian, Chelsea way, instead of the uncomfortably close-packed little chairs of the New Chenil Galleries.

I gathered that this entertainment, or something like it, was given some years ago (I must have missed it), and that it 'shocked Mr Noel Coward'; but whether this disturbing sentence in the advertisement was meant as a criticism of the entertainment or an epitaph upon Mr Coward I cannot say. There were one or two things in the show with which one might legitimately feel bored, but nothing to shock anyone. Some one (was it Osbert?) declaimed Miss Sitwell's poems through a megaphone placed in the mouth of a big face painted, half in white, half in pink, on the curtain, while a small orchestra, also behind the scenes, poured out the music of Mr W. T. Walton. How much I enjoyed the fun may be estimated from the fact that I—a critic—actually not only stayed to the end but added my voice and my umbrella to the clamour for encores of the best 'items' long after the official proceedings were finished.

Mr Sitwell, in his prefatory remarks, half hinted, apologetic-ally, that the speaker of the words might not be able to get them all 'over', but that if we happened to m ss any of them there was always the music to fall back upon. His scruples were unnecessary. It is true that against the jolly stridencies of Mr Walton's scoring what we got from the megaphone was often sound rather than sense, but for my part I felt that one or two of the poems were rather improved than otherwise by our not being able to catch the words. We got the essential things all right, such as—

> 'Or the sound of the onycha
> When the phoca has the pica
> In the palace of the Queen Chinee!'

(from the 'Trio for Two Cats and a Trombone'). But really the words mattered very little, in the majority of cases, as against the music.

The experience was another illustration of how necessary it is to find the right instrument for a tune, in poetry as in music. If I have missed, in my study, the inner meaning of some of Miss Sitwell's ingeniously wrought verses, it was because in my innocence I read them as I would read ordinary poetry. Mr Osbert Sitwell (if it were he at the back of the megaphone), showed me that they really demand a method of reading of their own. Get Kreisler to play one of Paul Whiteman's shirt. sleeves tunes on his violin, and the tune will sound nothing. Hear the free-and-easy thing on the trombone or the baritone saxophone and you are bound to admit that it has its qualities and its virtues; with tunes, as with people, the clothes are almost as important as what is inside them. Now when I read this of Miss Sitwell's:—

> 'Long steel grass—
> The white soldiers pass—
> The light is braying like an ass.
> See
> The tall Spanish jade
> With hair black as nightshade
> Worn as a cockade!
> Flee
> Her eyes' gasconade
> And her gown's parade
> (As stiff as a brigade).
> Tee-hee!'

or this—

> 'Beside the castanetted sea
> Where stalks Il Capitaneo
> Swaggart braggodocio

Sword and moustachio—
He
Is green as a cassada
And his hair is an Armada,'

or this—

'When,
'Sir

Beelzebub called for his syllabub in the hotel at Hell,'
the device of the broken line misses fire with me, because I
am not used to that sort of thing in the poetry I was brought
up on. But when the megaphone bellows the words at me with
a sledgehammer insistence on the 'See', 'Flee', 'When', and
'Sir', I get the poet's idea, and, I must confess, enjoy it.

These, in fact, are saxophone tunes, not violin melodies,
and must be played on the right instrument, with the right
technique, and in the right spirit. The reciter brought out also
all sorts of queer delightful rhythms and cross rhythms and
unexpected stabbing accents that gave me, as a musician whose
trade is in these things and who therefore knows what's what
where they are concerned, a vast delight. It is all very well for
old-fashioned purists to say that poetry should not be read
through a megaphone. The answer is that the Sitwells know
what they are driving at better than we do, and that, beyond
a doubt, Tuesday's reading of some of these poems gave us a
delight in them that we had not previously felt. To hear Osbert
and the megaphone pounding out—

'THE
Trumpet and the drum,
And the martial cornet come
To make the people dumb—
But WE
Won't wait for sly-foot night'

with a rhythm and an accent like those of a military march,
was to see the poem—for the first time with many of us—from
the poet's point of view.

But the entertainment owed a great deal also to Mr Walton's
music. All I knew of this young man's before Tuesday was a
horrible quartet of his that was given at the Royal College

three or four years ago. On the strength of this, I take leave to dislike intensely Mr Walton's serious music—if, indeed, that quartet *was* serious and *was* music, both of which I doubt. But as a musical joker he is a jewel of the first water. Not all the 'Façade' music came off, it is true. Some of it was too imitative of the sort of thing we used to hear in the great days of about 1920, when M. Diaghileff was writing—or at all events signing—those wonderful letters to the papers in which a new scheme of musical values was foreshadowed, Beethoven and Brahms and Elgar being reduced to the status of mere straphangers by the Stravinskys and Saties and Prokofieffs and Milhauds of the new dawn. Here and there Mr Walton could be seen diving into that sequestered and now stagnant pool and coming up with bits of Stravinsky sticking in his honest English hair; indeed, now and then the music was so like Stravinsky that it might have been written by Eric Fogg.

But when the true-born Briton settled down to the true-born Briton's historic rôle of guying things that have a natural touch of absurdity about them he was, as the modern stylist would say, priceless. Here is obviously a humorous musical talent of the first order; nothing so good in the mock-serious line of music has been heard for a long time as the 'Valse', the 'Polka', the 'Jodelling Song', and 'I do like to be beside the seaside'; and the deft workmanship, especially in the orchestration, made the heart of the listening musician glad.

The curious thing was the happiness of the correspondence between all the factors of the affair; the music, the words, the megaphone, and the piquant phrasing of the lines by the reciter were as much bone of each other's bone and flesh of each other's flesh as the words and the music are of each other in 'Tristan' or 'Pelléas'. At its best, 'Façade' was the jolliest entertainment of the season. Mr Playfair ought to incorporate the four numbers I have mentioned in 'Riverside Nights'. And Mr Walton ought to seek out a librettist after his own heart and give us a little musical comedy in the jazz style.

A NOTE ON DELIUS

10th November 1929

No composer who has ever lived being everybody's composer, I should not be at all surprised to be told that there are people who do not like Delius's music. There is room in this infinite universe for all varieties of taste. So long as people trust simply to their sensitised plates, regardless of whether the plate has had any special preparation for a particular piece of photography or indeed has any more natural capacity for taking an image faithfully than a dinner plate has, we must be prepared for all sorts of opinions upon the same subject, and learn to look upon them all with an amused philosophical detachment. As we were leaving Queen's Hall the other evening after a performance of the 'Mass of Life' that had moved many of us as no other concert experience has done for many a day, a young lady was heard to remark languidly to her companion, 'Gives you the dem creeps, doesn't it?' Evidently a sensitised plate can in some cases register only desensitised platitude.

If some people are blind to what others of us regard as the extraordinary beauty of Delius's music, we must just agree to differ on a matter on which there is no possibility of our ever coming to an agreement. But when these or other people keep assuring us that the music of Delius is all alike, discussion of a sort becomes possible, because here we are dealing with facts. No one would seek to deny that Delius has a partiality for certain harmonic progressions. These are called his mannerisms; and because even the casual listener is conscious of the frequent appearance of the same generic formula (for that is what a mannerism is), he is inclined, in his haste, to see only the formula and miss the manifold uses to which the formula is put. I can readily understand some people declaring that they cannot perceive any distinction between this work of Delius and that: I would merely point out that the inability to perceive a distinction is no proof that the distinction does not exist. It is all a matter of natural fineness of apprehension plus extent of experience. To make use of an old illustration, to the townsman all the faces in a flock are alike, whereas to the shepherd they are all different. I make bold to say that this inability to see the fine shades of distinction between one Delius work and another is a sure proof that the objector does not know his Delius apart from chance contact with him in the concert room.

The tables can easily be turned on these objectors. In the first place, our experiences of poetry show us that a writer may have the most pronounced of 'manners' and yet, within this manner, turn out no two works that are really alike. If we concentrate only on the externals of the Browning idiom, for instance, we merely perceive that it is the same in one work after another. But the reader who should assert that, because the Cardinal Ogniben of 'A Soul's Tragedy' speaks the same rather peculiar language as the old Pope in 'The Ring and the Book', the two characters say only the same thing, would simply write himself down an ass. And to anyone who has steeped himself in Delius there is something very foolish about the theory that because a composer has a language markedly his own he can say only a mere half-dozen things in it.

A little modesty on the part of these good people would not be amiss. They might reflect upon the obvious fact that others of us can listen with increasing interest to concert after concert of Delius's music. We have no more liking for being bored than they have; and it is surely a fair presumption that if one Delius work were very much like another our interest in him would soon die out. Is it too much to ask them to believe that although *they* cannot get below the external similarity of the language to the variety of things that is being said in this language others of us can, much to our delight? Is it strictly modest of them to elevate their own impercipience to the rank of a norm for more discriminating ears? Because, to their unskilled eye, ten fabrics in blue look all very much alike, must they force their crude opinion on the trained dyeing chemist who can perceive ten well-defined tints in them, and give each of the tints a distinguishing name or number?

In the second place, granted that Delius has a language of his own that is manifestly much the same, in its externals, in most of his works, how does he differ in this respect, we may

ask, from any other composer? The objector will say that the
proposition is not true, or not true to anything like the same
extent, of any other composer. I venture to assure him that he
is quite wrong. Here again he is merely arguing from his own
lack of perception. For some years I have been carrying out
an intensive analysis of the idioms of composers that has yielded
some curious and astonishing results. I have no hesitation in
saying that there is not a single composer who is not, in the
last resort, simply a machine unconsciously reproducing the
same basic formulae in work after work. That these formulae
have not been generally perceived is only another proof of
how musical criticism has failed at the very rudiments of its
job because, in its childish vanity, it has aimed at scaling the
heights before it has made a proper survey of the foundations.
We critics have been so preoccupied with our naive reactions to
a composer and with the equally naive attempt to persuade
other people that if they react to him differently from us they
are wrong, that we have never given any attention to what it is
in a particular composer's mind that goes a long way towards
making his music what it is.

So far as the main texture and the ordonance of his music
are concerned, every composer is merely a bundle of a dozen
or so constantly recurring formulae. This is not a matter of
conjecture: it is a plain fact that can be proved up to the hilt by
quotation. I would explain it in this way: in its subconscious
depths the human mind is, to a large extent, a machine, and
the machine, in order to economise energy, unconsciously
settles upon certain lines of least resistance; the same emergency
arising, as it is always doing in one work and another, the
machine applies to it the same formula, modified according to
the circumstances of the moment, and generally so subtly
modified that for generation after generation millions of
listeners have never even suspected its presence.

When, therefore, someone tells me that when he is listening to
Delius in the mass he is conscious of the same formula, manner,
mannerism—call it what you like—recurring again and again,
my reply is that I go through precisely the same experience
when I am listening to Beethoven, Wagner, Brahms,
Chopin, Weber, Schubert, Schumann, Grieg, Mozart, Elgar,

Strauss, and other composers. What the anti-Delian imagines to be a characteristic of Delius *qua* Delius is only a characteristic of him and others *qua* composer. (In no two composers, by the way, are the formulae the same, which is a very remarkable fact when we consider that there are only twelve notes in a chromatic octave.)

BACH AND BAROQUE

7th January 1934

THE game of comparing composers with poets or painters does not seem so popular as it used to be; but it might be worth some one's while to get together a collection of these supposed analogies, if only to illustrate the change in taste from one generation to another. Some of the judgments of our forefathers are really beyond comprehension today. Ask a dozen cultured people now to which painter they would compare Rossini, and while the whole twelve replies might be different, it is pretty safe to assume that none of them would be 'Titian'; yet it was to Titian that Liszt, expressing no doubt the general opinion of his epoch, compared Rossini! One or two of these old comparisons still give us occasion for thought—such as David Friedrich Strauss's description of Gluck as 'the Lessing of the opera'; but as a rule they merely make the modern reader smile.

There used to be one comparison that everyone thought perfectly safe, that of Mozart and Raphael. That was well enough in the days when all sorts of excellent people thought the good Raphael to be the greatest of painters. But would the comparison of Mozart and Raphael be taken nowadays as the highest compliment conceivable to the former? A modern critic assures us that

> Raphael, the marvellous creator of images, was a mediocre colourist . . . and . . . his drawing was often commonplace and nerveless. There is no picture by him in which an impartial critic may not find loose, inaccurate, and inexpressive contours. . . . Not without reason has the decadence of art been dated from the apogee of Raphael's glory. The worship of Raphael, 'the divine painter', has had its day. His works must now be analysed and judged one by one, not as those of a god in the form of a painter, but as the creations of an artist of genius, fallible like the rest of mankind, and deified by irresponsible enthusiasm. All that is truly great in his art

can but gain by being studied critically, not in the spirit of depreciation, but, on the other hand, without a blind determination to admire at any price.

The day may yet come when even Mozart will be studied critically and rationally along the lines thus laid down by Salomon Reinach for the study of Raphael. That the conventional Mozart-Raphael analogy still holds sway, however, in many minds—not in the modern critical but in the ancient adoring sense—is shown by its cropping up in one of the articles in the recent 'Mozart' number of the 'Revue Musicale'.

Still, there is a good deal to be said for these comparisons of musicians and artists, if only we do not carry them too far. No one composer is the precise and complete analogy to any one artist; but there may be one factor in a composer's make-up that brings him into line with a similar factor in the make-up of some painter or sculptor or other. If I were asked to name the artistic equivalent to Bach, I should plump for Bernini and some dozen or two other leading lights of baroque art. The comparison may cause some readers to raise their eyebrows, but that, I venture to suggest, will only be because they have studied critically and complementally neither Bach nor baroque.

There are, as a matter of fact, two or three Bachs, that seemingly have hardly any connection with each other. The general public knows, for the most part, only what I have called the jigging, jogging, Bach; it does not realise that the works of Bach that give it so much naive pleasure are merely the small talk of a mighty mind, the gay, airy, neatly shopfinished things—or nothings—that any good talker, desirous only of amusing himself and coming down for the moment to the intellectual level of his listeners, can toss out of his sleeve with the utmost ease between the soup and the fish. Of the greater and infinitely more fascinating Bach, the Bach of the Passions, the cantatas, and the chorale preludes, the general public knows next to nothing. And this is the Bach who turns out, on careful examination, to have the closest analogies with certain aspects of baroque.

Baroque is not a phenomenon of the seventeenth and eighteenth centuries alone. It is a recurrent phenomenon in art: the ancient Greeks had their baroque. It is something that always happens when two main factors coincide in point of time—a great store of technique, transmitted and personal, and an enormous heightening of sensibility. When this occurs we get, on the one hand, an insistence, that sometimes becomes exaggerated, on images of spiritual tension and suffering, on the other hand a kind of lust of technique, that shows itself in the elaboration, sometimes the over-elaboration, of one favourite feature of the creator's art.

It is somewhat astonishing that no writer, so far as my own reading goes, has pointed out the many analogies between the art of Bach and that of the masters of baroque. This is probably because students of music are as a rule too much occupied with their own problems to make an intensive study of other branches of art, while the students of pictorial and plastic art, though as a rule they have a method far superior to that of the average writer on music, necessarily lack the detailed knowledge of music that would enable them to apply their conclusions to the sister art. But occasionally they make a really good shot, as when the German art-historian, August Mayer, draws a comparison between the baroque music of Gluck and the Spanish baroque sculptor Gregorio Fernández (Hernandez.)

I think I have already pointed out that had 'musical criticism' existed in the days of Bach, he would have been solemnly censured in all the papers for two 'faults', an occasional over-insistence, in his harmonies, on images of spiritual suffering, and a tendency to over-elaborate his cadences for the sheer joy, as we may perhaps put it, of spreading himself. Fortunately for him, 'musical criticism' had in his days not yet attained to the full glory of puerility it has achieved in ours; so that when we now, some two centuries later, become aware of these qualities in his art, we do not react against them on the ground that they are signs of a deplorable 'decadence', but survey them and study them with dispassionate interest as phenomena that are sure to crop up, at some stage or other, in the course of the development of every art. Bach's harmonic over-intensity under the stress of some image of religious suffering or ecstasy finds a thousand analogies in the religious pictures and statues of the masters of baroque; while his elaborate cadences seem to me the perfect analogy, in music, to that luxury in the treatment of drapery that is so marked a characteristic in Bernini and others. (It was a noticeable characteristic also, by the way, of some of the sculpture of the Hellenistic period: and the same basic impulses repeat themselves in all the arts in some generation or other).

The truth is that there was a good deal more of the potential opera composer in Bach than is generally supposed. He would not work specifically in that genre because opera as it then was offered too few opportunities for art so complex as his. But opera was everywhere in the air at that time, and it half-unconsciously influenced many writers and musicians who, for one reason and another, were barred from direct traffic with the suspicious thing. Neumeister, who set a new fashion in cantata texts—Bach set several of them to music—expressly laid it down that the cantata was 'part of an opera'. The growing tendency among church composers to import dramatic methods into religious music aroused a good deal of opposition at that time; and Spitta rightly draws attention to the close analogy between 'the endeavour to express personal emotion on the boards of a theatre' and the 'transcendental subjectivity' of much of the poetry of the Pietists. In a thousand instances in his cantatas and Passions and chorale preludes Bach pays tribute, in his own way, to the heightened nervous sensibility that was then seeking its outlet in opera, as it had formerly done in baroque painting and sculpture.

Corresponding analogies might be worked out between certain aspects of the art of Hugo Wolf and the phase of Greek sculpture that is represented by Scopas and his followers. Wolf's insistence, in his more tragic songs, upon the utmost harmonic poignancy is paralleled by the tension in Scopas's faces, their fixed intensity of gaze. It would not be in the least fanciful to say that in each case the effect is obtained by much the same means, regard being had to the difference between the natures of the two arts: 'Wolf's minor ninth does for his tragic music just what Scopas did for his agonised faces by deepening the eye socket, and by that heavy fold of flesh over the outer corner of the eye that he so frequently uses to get an effect of tense concentration.

A whole book, indeed, might be written on the analogies between the music of Wolf and certain phenomena in the later developments of Greek sculpture. But here, as everywhere else, we must beware of wholesale analogies of the type that delighted the simpler sense of our fathers. No one composer corresponds so completely to any one painter or sculptor as to justify our calling him the This or That of music. The Wolf of 'Mühvoll komm' ich und beladen' is true Scopas; but we must find another analogy for the Wolf of 'Mögen alle bösen Zungen.' Similarly, while there is a good deal of rococo in Mozart, and a good deal that would justify us in regarding him as the musical equivalent of Watteau, there is also a good deal in his music for which we must find a very different analogy.

DELIUS:

THE END OF A CHAPTER IN MUSIC

17th June 1934

ELGAR, Holst, and now Delius! This is a year of mourning for English music. If the public, as distinct from one's private, grief is less poignant in the case of Delius than in those of the other two, it is because we had already realised that his activity was at an end. Elgar's mind, at the time of his death, was working eagerly not only upon his third symphony but upon the opera he had had on hand for so many years; and there is no knowing what might still have come from a mind so penetrating and boldly speculative as that of Holst. But in Delius's case, though his mind remained astonishingly strong until quite recently, the physical handicap became, in the end, more than he or any man could overcome.

Zur Ruh, zur Ruh, ihr müden Glieder!
Schliesst fest euch zu, ihr Augenlider!

Delius was one of those rare composers whom it is impossible to fit into any of the usual convenient categories: from first to last he was purely and wholly himself. One looks in vain in his music for any 'influence' whatever; at most we can detect occasionally a slight similarity between some of his harmonic progressions and those of Grieg, but even here it is not a matter of actual influence, but of a certain congenital correspondence between the two minds in this one small corner of music. For good or for ill, Delius was barred by his very constitution from either profiting by or being damaged by the example of any of his predecessors or contemporaries. Though he studied for a time at Leipzig, Leipzig left nothing whatever of its characteristic mark upon him. Like Berlioz, he must have worked hard during his formative days in a way entirely his own, guided by a sure instinct of what it was necessary for him to take over from tradition in the way of technique, and what had better be rejected as being finally unassimilable by a mind like his, and inapplicable to purposes like his.

It is true that here and there his music prompts the thought that in casting from him what he felt to be alien to him in the conventional technique he threw away also something by which, could he have made the essence if not the doctrine of it part of himself, his own technique might have profited. There are occasions, that is to say, especially in his earlier work on a large scale, when we feel that his hand is not quite subdued to the medium in which it is working, when the notes do not represent with perfect accuracy what it was in his mind to say. But one finally decides that he was right in refusing at all costs the assistance of the standard recipes—the use of which Brahms so liberally permitted himself when he was in a temporary structural difficulty—and in preferring to set down his dreams in his own way, even at the risk of an occasional awkwardness or lack of ideal clearness. Minds like his and Berlioz's have to pay the penalty of their originality; they have not only to find their own individual expression but create for themselves their own individual forms. In Delius's case the problem soon resolved itself into an intensive exploration of his own inner world as it was in the beginning, rather than a spatial enlargement of that world.

No two minds could be more different in orientation than his and Brahms's; but in one respect they were curiously alike. Sink a shaft into any two or three of Brahms's works, dating from his first, his middle, and his last period, and you come upon the same metal. There are minds, such as that of Wagner, that changed their tissue so much in the course of the years that one can hardly believe that their first and their last works were written by the same man. There are other minds, such as that of Brahms, that appear to be full-formed from the first; as life's spiritual experience works upon them they do indeed fill the native mould with a substance of ever greater strength and beauty, but in essence both the mould and the filling remain to to the end what they were at the beginning. So it was with Delius. His music is sometimes reproached with being the same in one work after another. To some extent this is true; the same rhythms, the same harmonies, the same exquisite washes of colour, recur again and again: sometimes, even, he unconsciously repeats himself literally, a certain passage in

'A Mass of Life', for instance, being an almost literal reproduction of one in 'Sea Drift'. But with Delius, as with Brahms, though the music remains superficially the same throughout the years, its inner tissue and timbre and clang are subtly modified in one work after another. In Delius's case, perhaps, one requires a special sensibility, and considerable acquaintance with the music, before these fine shades of distinction between works that to the casual ear sound very much alike can be distinguished; but of their existence there can be no doubt.

His music is full of paradoxes. One's first impression of some of it is that it is formless: later one discovers that it has a form, and a perfectly adequate form, of its own. In this respect posterity will do him more justice than is possible to the ordinary listener of today, who has been herded by precept and example into confusing truly organic musical form with the merely schematic: some day it will be recognised that a work like 'Paris', in which the nature and the pressure of the thinking evolve their own perfectly congruent shape and articulation from the inside, instead of docilely accepting a standardised scheme applied to the music from the outside, represents a higher achievement in form than is to be met with in many a dozen 'classical' symphonies.

Another paradox is that while his music seems to glide along with limbs relaxed, it is often, in reality, extraordinarily vigorous, as many a page in 'A Mass of Life' testifies. It is simply that in music of this kind, as in the bodies of the cat tribe, the muscles can put forth the maximum of energy with the minimum of visible effort. Delius's mind in general was one of exceptional strength; and only listeners who are unable to get past the smoothness of the texture of his music to the thought that is functioning within can be under any illusion as to the same strength being there in his music.

If his mind, from first to last, moved within an orbit that seems limited in comparison with that of minds like Wagner's or Beethoven's, it gradually developed the maximum of light and heat within its own orbit. A penetrating and realistic thinker in matters of the intellect, as a musical artist his whole life was devoted to the progressive realisation, in ever clearer forms and ever more poignant expression, of the one primal ideal of beauty, a beauty that is eager in the earlier works, passionate and richly coloured in those of his middle period, and with the sadness of autumn in it in some of his latest works, where he seems to recognise regretfully at last, as we must all do, that this hard world is not to be shaped by the artist and dreamer to his heart's desire. In the music of his final period, with its poignant nostalgia for a beauty that is fast vanishing from the earth, we hear, as in no other music but that of Mahler's, 'the sunset cry of wounded kings', the last regretful murmuring of ancient talismans which, in its strange blend of credulity and negation, the distracted new world has for the time being rejected.

With the death of Delius there has died a world the corresponding loveliness to which it will be a long time before humanity can create for itself again. It may be that, as some think, we are now in the first hour before a new dawn in music. But that hour is grey and chilly: and those of us who have been drunk with the beauty and the glory of the sunset of civilisation as we knew it must find our consolation in the melting colours of the cloud-shapes of the music of this last great representative of that old dead world. Delius has summed it all up for us in his moving setting of the no less moving words that Nietzsche puts into the mouth of his Zarathustra:

> O man! Take heed!
> What saith deep midnight's voice indeed?
> 'I slept my sleep—,
> 'From deepest dream I've woke, and plead:—
> 'The world is deep.
> 'And deeper than the day could read.
> 'Deep is its woe—,
> 'Joy deeper still than grief can be:
> 'Woe saith: Hence! Go!
> 'But joys all want eternity—,
> '—Want deep, profound eternity!'

BACH AND HANDEL:

PAST AND PRESENT VIEWS

3rd March 1935

W<small>HEN</small> the examining counsel asked the witness how he could be so sure that the exact distance from point A to point B was so many feet so many inches, he received the answer that he had measured it. Asked why he had measured it, witness replied, 'Because I knew some damned fool or other would ask me.' The musical world is supposed to be frightfully agitated just now—though I have seen no striking evidence of it myself so far—over the fact that if Handel and Bach were still alive they would now be 250 years old, Handel having been born on February 23rd, 1685, and Bach on March 21st. On occasions like this we journalists are of course expected to say something. For my part I can see no more and no less reason for writing about a composer on his birthday than for writing about him on any other day. If then I follow the example of my colleagues and take Bach and Handel for my subject today, it is only because I know that if I don't, some intelligent person or other is sure to write and ask me why.

I was mildly amused a little while ago to read that Bach had had a fine innings lately and it was now time that Handel went to the wicket. That remark, I fancy, was prompted by too close a study of the Promenade Concerts programmes during the last few years. But the Promenades, excellent institution though they are in their way, are not the universe, or even the British Isles: and if we run a line through the musical life of this country as a whole during the last two hundred years or so, I think we shall find that it is Handel who has always had the greater public vogue. He has always been, and probably always will be, the one of the pair who can contribute most to the greatest happiness of the greatest number. On the other hand, if we may judge from the specialist literature on the subject, it is Bach who keeps the minds of thoughtful musicians working

118

hardest and most constantly. What I call specialist musical literature—i.e., the study by sensitive experts of the constitution and the working of a composer's mind, as distinguished from the dilettante literature of the rapturous record of sensitised-plate reactions—is relatively small in the case of Handel; whereas in the case of Bach it is not only already large but increasing every year. About the 'Art of Fugue', for example, which is hardly a 'work' at all in the popular sense of the term, the last few years alone have seen the production of an astonishing quantity of literature, culminating in Erich Schwebsch's volume of 350 pages (1931). We might sum it all up, perhaps, by saying that Handel will always be the public's musician, one of the greatest and most enjoyable of composers, while Bach is and will always be the musician's musician.

In spite of the fact that the two were born in the same year, lived for practically the same length of time, and, Handel's operas apart, employed much the same vocabulary, forms, and technical means, their minds show more differences than resemblances. This fact is not, as is generally supposed, the discovery of today. Our great-grandfathers were perfectly conscious of it; indeed, when we read the discussions of the pair in the musical literature of the last years of the eighteenth century or the first years of the nineteenth, we feel that there is little that is essential to be added to them today. We can fill in the picture with a thousand fresh details, but the main outlines of it were virtually settled long ago. Perhaps our grandfathers were even more acutely conscious of the fundamental differences between the mind of Bach and that of Handel than the average concert-goer today is, after his much wider experience of the two.

During the last few years more than one investigator has given intensive study to the analogies between Bach's music and Gothic architecture. But Weber, although he could not have known one-tenth of the works of Bach that are familiar to us today, not only hit upon that analogy but anticipated the later critical thesis that Bach is more of a 'romantic' than Handel. Discussing these two 'giant minds', as he calls them, in an article of 1821, Weber says that they are basically so different that they seem to belong to different epochs. 'Bach's individuality was really romantic, fundamentally German, contrasting with

Handel's more antique grandeur'. He puts forward as a vital characteristic of Bach's style not only the purity and logic of his linear counterpoint, but the extraordinary variety and subtlety of his rhythms within the parts—a point upon which the latest research and stylistic analysis have especially concentrated. (Handel's rhythms are also varied and subtle, but only melodically, in the upper line of a harmony, not in every limb and fragment of a polyphonic tissue as is the case with Bach.) Weber goes on to compare Bach's music with 'a Gothic cathedral'.

Rochlitz, in an article published in book form in 1832, though seemingly written some years before then, makes a good point when he compares Handel's music with the art of Rubens at his best, and Bach's with that of Dürer. He is as conscious as any of us today that Handel's gaze was turned more outward and Bach's more inward: Handel makes us, he says, see the thing as he saw it, while Bach makes us live it as he had lived it. These ancients saw as clearly as any expert of today that the two men's minds differed fundamentally in their attitude towards polyphony. Handel, with the public listener always in his mind's eye, does not insist upon his counterpoint after the moment when he conceives it would be a little irksome for the average man to follow him (a point that is implicit in Hawkins's description of Handel's improvisation at the organ): Bach, with no public to think of, lets the inner logic of his subjects have its own way, purely for their own sake, for his, and for those after him who can delight, after enthusiastic and painstaking study, in the musical result. People like Rochlitz were as well aware as any of us today that there was something in Bach's mind that made it, for all time, the epitome of the musical mind at its most truly musical: *this*, we say as we examine this or that great work of his, is how music might write itself if no human apparatus were needed between the first conception and the final result.

Hence it comes about that we listen to Bach and Handel today in altogether different ways. If a Handel work is not first-rate we just leave it on one side and pass on to another of his that is; the degree of aesthetic pleasure given us is the determining factor. But there are dozens of Bach works which, though they communicate no particular aesthetic pleasure in the commoner sense of that term, still draw us to them again and again. Few of the fugues in the 'Art of Fugue' are as 'pleasing' to the ordinary listener as those in the 'Forty-eight' or those for the organ; but all the same we take down from our shelves the 'Art of Fugue' many more times than we do any of the Handel fugues, splendid as some of these are. It is not that we take a dry-as-dust interest in Bach's technique for its own sake; it is simply that we feel again and again that here the spirit of music is realising itself according to its own inexorable inner necessity; and the delighted feeling that this perception gives us is something that on occasion can transcend 'aesthetic' enjoyment as the man in the street conceives it.

It is impossible, perhaps, to make the man in the street see what it is in Bach that endlessly absorbs and thrills the musician; it is difficult, indeed, to express it in words to one's own satisfaction. But all the same it is there, and it is this that accounts for the vast literature devoted to Bach analysis. That analysis is not mere analytical chemistry for its own dry laboratory sake: it is the effort of the musical mind within us to penetrate to the profoundest secrets of the musical mind as its most musical.

Brahms was a subscriber to the editions of both the big Handel and the big Bach Societies. When a new volume of the former arrived, he would turn the pages and say 'This is very interesting; I must go through it as soon as possible.' But when a Bach volume arrived he would put aside everything else, neglect every engagement, until he had studied it through and through. The story serves as a good illustration of the attitude of the profounder musical mind everywhere and in all epochs towards the two giants; Wagner, again, in his last years, constantly played Bach or had Bach played to him. We go to the two men for two quite different things; but for all the beauty, the splendour, the grandeur, the humanity that endear Handel to us, it is Bach who holds us with a spell the potency of which increases with the years.

DELIUS AND THE OPERA:

A QUEST FOR THE IMPOSSIBLE?

29th September 1935

At Covent Garden last Monday, during the intervals and at the end of the performance, everyone was saying that 'Koanga' was undramatic and that Delius had little talent for opera. The general truth of these propositions cannot be disputed. Everything in Delius's musical make-up that made him what he was, with all his qualities and all his defects, ran counter to the ordinary conception of opera. In spite of the fact that here and there in 'Sea Drift', in the 'Mass of Life', and in certain other works he has given us some of the most moving interpenetrations of words and music that the history of the art can show, it remains true that, speaking generally, he had virtually no feeling for words. Again and again, in work after work, he sets the teeth of the sensitive listener on edge with his awkward handling of words. It will be said, of course, in some quarters, that where music is concerned the words do not greatly matter. The answer to that easy-going proposition is that there is no law to compel a composer to take words as the starting-point and the inspiration of his music, but that if he chooses to do so he will naturally be expected to observe certain rules of the game. If he persistently shapes his phrases in such a way that the accents and the rhythms and the rise and fall of his music run counter to the very life of the words, he must not complain if sometimes he brings a grimace to the face of his hearers.

Delius's well-known mannerisms as a musician are particularly unpropitious for the setting of words. A glance at random at almost any page of 'Koanga' will show the backbone of the verbal phrases being broken or weakened by the persistent bias of the composer's mind towards certain fixed formulae of musical accent, rhythm, harmony, and contour. No other composer has ever 'declaimed' so badly as Delius: rarely can a sentence that has been set to music by him be sung as one would speak it. The music imposes its own accent, rhythm, and articulation upon it; and as these, as everyone recognises, are somewhat standardised in Delius, the result is that not only are the words themselves mishandled, but there emerges next to nothing of the variety of impression that character in action ought to give us on the stage. In 'Koanga', for instance, not only do all the characters talk very much alike, but the same character expresses himself in much the same way in all circumstances. It is useless to reply that all Wagnerian characters speak Wagner's special idiom, all Mozartian or Straussian characters an idiom that is unmistakably Mozart or Strauss. That must be granted: but the fact remains that within the limitations of a style marked out for them by their own personalities these composers do succeed in making one stage character sound different from another. Delius does not succeed in doing so.

His lack of a sense of the theatre is shown in various other ways. He was so uncritical of the words he was setting that he seems to have accepted anything that a librettist put before him. It never occurred to him that his music would be handicapped from the commencement by the characters talking as they would never talk in life or in literature worthy of the name, but only in the jargon that was thought to be *de rigueur* in opera a generation or two ago. We do not know, of course, to what extent the just-published text of 'Koanga' has been 'revised' by other hands: but in the absence of any definite information on that point we must assume that Delius really thought, in company with his librettist, that negro slaves on an American cotton plantation would say, 'The dawn begins to gild the East. Each cabin door opens to greet the strident (*sic*) call. The world resumes again its old unchanging round', and so on: or again, when they have been awakened from sleep a second time, 'Once again the weary sun ascends from pallid ocean bed.' Nor would any composer with a sense of the theatre, dealing with a subject from real life in which the only clue to the psychological motivation of the characters is what they say about themselves and each other, set half-a-dozen people singing different things at the same time in different rhythms, with the result that all we hear is a web of rich sound with no definite meaning.

The cases of the quintet in the 'Meistersinger' and the trio in the 'Rosenkavalier' are not on all fours with this general procedure of Delius. The really dramatic composer knows precisely why, for a minute or two, he departs from the plain commonsense rule in these matters: he does so deliberately, in order to bring the action and the psychology to a momentary head, and the overriding result justifies him, even in the theatre. The trouble with Delius is, in the first place, that these departures from dramatic verisimilitude are the outcome not of a superior musical-dramatic sense but of the total lack of that sense, and in the second place that, never having been able to visualise in his study the totality of the thing as it would reveal itself on the stage, he sometimes lands himself in a situation that is not merely non-dramatic but downright comic. The cardinal example of this is the episode in which Palmyra, Clotilda, Perez, Koanga, Martinez, and a four-part chorus of negroes in the fields—plus, of course, the orchestra —unite in an ensemble in which each of the principal characters is given words of his own that are intended to reveal his own motives and reactions. The result of it all is that we do not catch a single word of what they are saying, but when the soloists suddenly lapse into silence we hear the negroes informing us—as if this had been the essence of the whole matter— that 'Now we may put scythe and sickle away, for the dinner-bell is ringing!'

Delius's congenital helplessness in stage matters is shown in various other ways. 'Koanga' is too long for a short opera and too short for a long one: consequently as the audience has to be given the feeling that it is getting its money's worth in the shape of a full evening's entertainment, the time has to be spun out with extraneous orchestral matter (presumably from other works of his); which has the double effect of thinning out the tenuous stage action still further and of making the audience feel at the end that some of the music it liked best had nothing to do with the drama.

To make out a general case against Delius as a dramatist, then, is easy. But when we have said all we can say along these lines we have perhaps only touched the surface of the matter. A more sympathetic and perhaps more discerning view of it all would be that Delius's failure is due to his having been reaching out all his life to a new dramatic form germane to his genius, without ever succeeding in discovering quite what that form would have to be. Ordinary dramatic expression of character or painting of situation was in the main beyond him: in his art, as in his life, he was much too self-centred for that. But in his own way he certainly had an interest in character and situation; and the problem for him was to find a dramatic, or quasi-dramatic, form that would enable him to deal with these in his own peculiar way. By the very build of his brain he was incapacitated from attaining much variety of musical idiom, though he could give an astonishing number of facets to the idiom that was personal to him. He could never get outside himself, never project himself, as the more objective dramatist necessarily has to do; with him, man, like nature, had always to be shown as he appeared to Delius.

He is therefore in his real element in drama only when he can talk *in propria persona* about a vital matter instead of making the protagonists speak for themselves. The best thing in 'The Village Romeo and Juliet' is that exquisite intermezzo in which Delius shows us his young lovers not in action but as a pretext for his own tender and pitiful musing upon them. In 'Koanga' he begins with a prologue and ends with an epilogue in which Uncle Joe and his listeners first talk of the drama-to-come and then reflect upon it. That this is 'bad theatre' we all admit: but it is good Delius. He may not be able to show us Koanga and Palmyra convincingly upon the stage: but when he himself pours out upon them and us the flood of his sensitive brooding upon them we feel that purification of the soul by pity which was, of course, his real purpose in taking up this drama, but the full realisation of which was possible to him only in his own way, not in the ordinary way of the theatre.

He found, for once, something like the material and the form that enabled him to express himself dramatically in his own way—in his 'Fennimore and Gerda'. Here the action of Jacobsen's novel ('Niels Lhyne') is cast into eleven short scenes, each lasting no more than a few minutes. Economic and other conditions of the theatre make the work practically impossible, of course. If, however, it could be given in a production in the half-mystical style suited to it, it would produce an extraordinary effect—at any rate on an audience of philosophers and poets. For here, at last, Delius found a form that allowed him to describe the inner drama of souls in his own way, a way that allowed him to accompany the characters in person, by means of his music (especially of his orchestral interludes), in each of the decisive episodes of their career. One finally comes to the conclusion that all his life he was groping towards a new type of musical drama, but that the problems with which it confronted him were beyond the capacity either of his librettists, his own genius, or the conventional theatre to solve.

SIBELIUS NO. 4:

ITS ENGLISH HISTORY

29th August 1937

THERE is no longer any reason to complain that Sibelius is 'neglected' in this country. The Promenade Concerts have always been a sure indication of the composers in whom the plain musical man has been most interested at any given moment; and not only do this year's programmes include each of Sibelius's seven symphonies, together with the violin concerto and several of the tone poems, but last Thursday, for, I believe, the first time in Promenade history, Sibelius had the whole concert to himself. Really to himself; for whereas the so-called Wagner or Beethoven or Brahms or Bach evenings are diluted, at any rate in the second half, by the works of all and sundry, on Thursday Sibelius had the field to himself from first to last with the 'Festivo' from the 'Scènes Historiques', two symphonies (the third and the fourth), the violin concerto, 'The Swan of Tuonela', and 'The Return of Lemminkainen'.

The truth is, however, that while Sibelius's vogue has grown rapidly during the last ten years he was never, all things considered, 'neglected' in England. Sir Henry Wood in London, and Sir Granville Bantock in Liverpool and Birmingham, were giving what were then his newest works a good thirty years ago; the first symphony, in fact, figured in a Promenade concert programme of 1903. Mrs Rosa Newmarch's informative booklet on him dates from about 1906. By 1907 Sibelius was so conscious of owing much to his English enthusiasts that he dedicated the score of his third symphony, which was finished about that time, to Sir Granville Bantock. The fourth symphony, finished in 1911, had a place of honour in the Birmingham Festival conducted by Sir Henry Wood in October, 1912; and the publishers were sufficiently confident of the interest that would be taken in it to bring out a brochure of fifteen pages, by Mrs Newmarch, dealing in considerable detail with the composer in general and the new work in particular. The novelty of idiom and above all the terseness of expression in the No. 4 necessarily gave our musical public something to think about; and then before either Sibelius could come forward with another major work or people could finish the digestion of the first four symphonies and some of the tone poems—all of which had been presented to them within some nine years—the war broke out.

It was some years before music quite got on its feet again in this country, and some further years before public opinion could steady itself after the wild theorising of the first post-war period; so that it was not until 1921 that London heard the fifth symphony. But Sibelius had now virtually to begin over again in England; and a few more years were required to establish him securely with a new generation of concert-goers. Conductors soon found that the first and second symphonies were not only easy to give but decidedly effect-making with any audience. Encouraged by this discovery that a Sibelius work was not only good music but good policy, they began to compete with each other in their attempts to be first with the Sibelius news. He quickly became a concert best-seller: the fifth, sixth, and seventh symphonies, 'Tapiola' and other works of his later period were given with reasonable frequency, considering the congested conditions of our concert life. The one major work of his that hung fire was the violin concerto, which, in its first form, dates from as long ago as 1903. (It was revised in 1905.) The responsibility for this neglect rested not with the public or the conductors but the star violinists, the majority of whom, for all the service they have been to the cause of contemporary music, might just as well have never been born. It was left to the musicians among the fiddlers, not to the stars, to discover the concerto. I myself heard it for the first time some ten years ago in Paris, when the solo part was taken by some player so unknown to fame of the Albert Hall type that I regret to say I cannot now remember his name. I believe it was Arthur Catterall who floated the concerto in this country. The trail thus having been blazed, the stars are now beginning to find that the work is worth their attention.

There can be no doubt that the cause of the temporary set-back in Sibelius's vogue was the coming of the war fast upon the heels of the production of the fourth symphony. That work was so different from any other of its type that it would have required, round about 1912, frequent hearings to familiarise listeners with what were at that time regarded as its startling novelties of idea and form; and frequent performances were of course made impossible by the war. The approach to the No. 4 would have been easier for the general public by way of the No. 5 (1915); but, as I have said, this was not given here until 1921. More frequent performances of Nos. 1, 2, and 3 would also have helped in the comprehension of No. 4; for there is really nothing in this that is not implicit, in one way or another, in the other symphonies, even down to the seventh. But in 1912 the No. 4 was rather a tough nut for the English to crack, partly because of its purely Finnish and Sibelian mentality. I remember that at one of the Birmingham rehearsals of the work a man whom I did not know seated himself beside me and looked curiously at my score, apparently in the hope that the evidence of his eyes might help to supply the understanding that had escaped him on the evidence of his ears alone. When the rehearsal was over he said to me, 'Queer stuff, isn't it?' I tried to point out to him that his difficulty, which I was sure would only be a temporary one, was that this music came from a different national- and culture-heredity from ours: 'it comes from Finland', I explained. 'Ah!' he said, with the air of one on whom the light has dawned: 'that's it: ah coom from Halifax myself.' Since that epoch, thanks entirely to Sibelius, the distance separating Halifax from Helsingfors has been appreciably diminished.

The No. 4 no longer has any terrors for even a 'popular' audience, for the first three symphonies on the one hand, and the last three on the other, have given every intelligent listener the clue to it. Sibelius does virtually nothing in the No. 4 that he does not do, in almost precisely the same terms, at the equivalent point in each of his major works. I have more than once hinted, in this column, that the essence of each composer's general procedure can be reduced, by analysis, to a few simple formulae: the constitutional bias of his mind makes him do practically the same thing again and again when he is confronted by much the same general idea to be expressed or much the same design to be built up. Composers, I find, are curiously sensitive about this matter when you begin to talk to them about it: some of them get very angry, others tighten their lips and take refuge in a dignified silence: apparently they think that if the thesis can be proved it will reduce them to the level of machines. As to the fact, however, there can be no dispute; the only difficulty in the way of establishing it to every reader's satisfaction is that in the case of each composer the demonstration would mean the quotation of some hundreds of musical examples. It is no use our pointing out to those of our personal friends who write music that, on the one hand, what is true of them is equally true of all the greatest classics —Beethoven in particular; and that on the other hand the same basic procedure is capable of so many modifications, and such subtle modifications, in practice that the ordinary music lover can listen to the great composers all his life without for a moment suspecting the subconscious operation in them of the law to which I have referred. Our friends, as I know from personal experience, are not to be propitiated.

Now the two composers whom I have found most constant, without knowing it, to a few fundamental formulae are Beethoven and Sibelius; and once you know the Sibelian formulae you have the main explanation of why the No. 4 was found rather baffling twenty-five years ago. Something in the constitution of his mind or in his spiritual experience just then impelled him to a titanic effort of concentration: the result was that at one point after another he either cut out altogether what would elsewhere have been preparatory matter or considerably curtailed it. I have space here for only one illustration. He is very fond of a procedure which, borrowing a term from the engraver's art, one might call cross-hatching—in music, an extensive repetition of rapid figures about one or more fixed points. The auditory effect, as I have implied, is very much the equivalent of the visual effect of cross-hatching. But when we come to ask ourselves the reason for this procedure we have to resort to another image—that of the propeller. Beethoven has a not dissimilar way of working up steam: he will sometimes repeat a little figure until by sheer repetition it has generated the energy he requires to launch his big motive. (The reader will find an example of this in the 'Egmont' overture, bars

125-134 counting backward from the final allegro con brio: to vary the simile once more, Beethoven needs a long run up to the wicket and several preliminary hand-flourishes before he can fling the ball—in this case his great main theme).

Sibelius's cross-hatching serves a similar purpose. It helps him to get up steam, as it were: out of this whirl of notes there comes in due time the big tune or the massive brass chords, much as the big ship gets fairly going after some beating about with its propellers. It is a point of manner that occasionally comes dangerously near mannerism; and it is not unlikely that when his music becomes thoroughly familiar to the ordinary listener the mannerism will in some places constitute a weak spot. It is part and parcel, however, of Sibelius's cast of mind; he invariably resorts to it in pretty well the same place for precisely the same purpose in one work after another. He puts it to varied and sometimes magnificent uses; but there are also indications here and there that he has consciously tried to rid himself of its tyranny over his mind, and in his greatest symphony, the No. 7, he gives us only occasional hints of it. In the No. 3 it is very prominent, less so in the No. 5, markedly so in the No. 6. In the No. 4 he seems to have made a convulsive effort to dispense with it, to evolve and link up his really vital material without its aid; and it is because here he so often lays one great stone directly upon another without the customary cement that the No. 4 makes demands upon the listener's concentration which the first hearers of it found rather excessive.

In one or two places in the No. 4, on the other hand, he is apt to confuse or disappoint the ordinary hearer by indulging for some time in this propeller work and then frustrating the expectation of the big tune that normally follows it and is the justification of it. In the first movement, for instance, a long preparation-piece of the kind I have described begins at Letter E of the score. It culminates, at Letter I, in one of those splendid lion-roars in the brass that are characteristic of Sibelius. But here he does not go on to his big tune as he almost invariably does elsewhere—in the finale of the No. 5, for example, where, after a long and increasing tension of very much the same type as that of the point just mentioned in the No. 4, he lets the engines out for all they are worth and sails grandly into the open sea. In the No. 4 he does not carry on in this way, but, after a second brass eruption, brings the movement to an end with less than twenty quiet bars. The procedure justifies itself, taking into consideration the movement as a whole; but undoubtedly the casual listener, especially if he has some acquaintance with the other orchestral works, feels that his expectation of something huge to come out of so much propeller work has been defeated. The No. 4, in fact, is of exceptional interest to the Sibelian student now in the light thrown on it by the No. 7 and 'Tapiola', where at last the composer attains, in a single movement, the drastic concentration at which he had been aiming in the earlier work.

THE MOST PATHETIC SYMPHONY:

TCHAIKOVSKY AND THE CONDUCTORS

3rd October 1937

THE announcement of Tchaikovsky's Pathetic Symphony in the programme of a Promenade Concert the other evening was a reminder of how seldom we hear that work nowadays. Some of us can still remember the sensation it caused at its first appearance. It was new in so many ways, both in form and in expression. A symphony that ended with a slow movement was a novelty: while the five-four movement created much the kind of excitement that the Indians must have felt when white— or relatively white—men first appeared on the shores of America.

In those days people could hardly listen to the music of the movement for its own sake, so preoccupied were they with the new and baffling problem of counting five: all round the concert hall could be seen men and women resolutely ticking off one, two, three, four, five: one, two, three, four, five, on one hand with the fingers of another; getting into difficulties and finding their fingers becoming all thumbs as soon as what seemed to be a strong beat came on the second note of the bar, instead of on the first as they had expected; hastily substituting the thumb for the first finger; discovering a couple of bars |later that their counting was all wrong; and finally giving up the stupendous problem in despair. Among the younger and more mathematic- ally minded enthusiasts there would be heated debates next day as to whether the five was two plus three or three plus two, or one plus four or four plus one, or, as another school of thought maintained, just plain five. Under the unaccustomed strain more than one powerful intellect tottered on its throne. Fortunately the problem was localised until it could be pretty well mastered: if, on top of the Tchaikovsky five-four, our audiences had been confronted just then with the eleven-four chorus in Rimsky-Korsakov's 'Sadko', the lunatic asylums of this country would have burst their walls.

It was not the five-four movement, however, that accounted for the attraction of the 'Pathetic' at that time. Towards that movement people mostly felt very much as the little boy in Arnold Bennett's story did in front of the painting of a lion in its cage: he used, it will be remembered, to come as near as he dared to touching the bars of the cage, more than half fearful that the lion would bite him. The five-four in any other world would probably have repelled as much as it attracted. What gave the Pathetic its enormous vogue was first of all the passion of pessimism that filled the first movement and the last. This was something new in music. Moreover, the composer had not only died within two or three weeks of the first performance of the symphony—an admirable strategic stroke on the part of any composer who wants popularity—but the word had gone round that he had committed suicide. The symphony was therefore 'a human document'. Even its title, 'The Pathetic', was an asset.

Then the long tragicomedy of the work began: it was soon to become pathetic in a way of which its composer had never dreamed. Writers with a vast knowledge of music made the remarkable discovery that its opening theme:

was very like that of Beethoven's 'Pathetic' sonata:

The reminiscence-hounds bayed as only they among canines can bay: what they overlooked was the simple fact that the supposed reminiscence was no reminiscence at all, but merely one more use of a grief-motive that is very common in modern music. It will be seen, for instance, at A in the following quotation from Tannhäuser's Pilgrimage:

Wagner's works, indeed, from the youthful F sharp minor piano Fantasia onwards, are full of it in its simplest as well as the most subtly sophisticated forms; it is the germ-idea, again, of the first of Brahms's Four Serious Songs. How completely the figure had taken possession of Tchaikovsky's imagination is shown incidentally by the way it reappears in an inner part in the second subject:

Tchaikovsky, in fact, being a very natural composer, who wrote just as he felt, had unconsciously packed his symphony with this and other 'natural' expressions of grief—the wailing descending theme, for instance. (The music of the last two or three hundred years is largely based on these 'natural' motives; a card index of them could easily be compiled and would be very instructive) And not only had he done this but he had marked his score with an amount of detail that showed how interested he was in what he was saying, and how much importance he attached to the 'message' of his music being made clear to the listener. (See, for example, how many marks of expression he has crowded into the few bars of No. 1 above.) His passion, his sincerity and his anxiety were his undoing. The strange fauna of 'star' conductors swooped on to the symphony like beasts of prey. It did not seem to strike more than one or two of them that what the symphony has to say is all contained in the music itself: they must needs overtrump every one of Tchaikovsky's trumps, dot all his i's, double-cross all his t's.

They plunged themselves, the work, and their audiences into a bath of blood and tears; never since the death of poor Cock Robin had there been such a sighin' and a sobbin'.

The end of it all might have been foreseen. The conductors disgusted sober people with the work; for the plain man, who does not read scores for himself, naturally assumed that all the sentimentality and vulgarity that the conductors put into the symphony were in the symphony itself. The Pathetic gradually became one of the bad jokes of the musical world, till finally those of us who knew it to be a masterpiece of its genre were driven to the resolution never to listen to it again if we could help it, but just to study it for ourselves in the quiet of our homes. In proportion as the memory of our dreadful experiences in the concert room faded we were able to see the thing as its creator had conceived it.

One of these days, perhaps, we shall hear it again precisely as it is written, without any of the changes of tempo and expression the majority of conductors inflict upon it or the grossness of their own sentiment which they read into it. Before many weeks are out I propose to suggest a plain and simple way by which those members of an audience who know a great work as it is, and who resent the humiliations it generally receives at the hands of conductors who are bent only on personal exhibitionism, can make their influence felt during the actual performance. I am going to suggest the formation of an S.P.C.C., and shall ask for the co-operation of all the younger people who really care about music. How necessary a Society of that kind is could be demonstrated from the plain facts of almost any performance we used to hear of the Pathetic.

Take, for instance, the case of the five-four movement. As the reader will remember, this falls into two main groups. The chief theme (A) is first of all stated at length in the major. Then comes a contrasting theme (B) in the minor. Towards the end of the development of this wailing theme Tchaikovsky begins to work into the tissue of it hints of A; till at last A takes full possession once more. It was the almost invariable practice of conductors to slow down, for 'expression's' sake, the tempo of B, sometimes to almost half the pace of A, regardless of the plain fact that Tchaikovsky intended both sections of the movement to proceed in the same tempo. The tempo marking at the commencement of the movement (allegro con grazia, crotchet 144) obviously applied to the whole of it, for there is not a single indication of any change in this respect from the first bar to the last. The only other marking in the movement is 'con dolcezza e flebile' at the head of B, and this is not in any sense whatever a tempo indication: it merely means 'sweetly and mournfully'. The result of the slowing down of section B was in the first place that the music here acquired a gross sentimentality that is really alien to it, and in the second place that when at last A is resumed the tempo had to be suddenly and irrationally quickened to something like twice the immediately preceding one.

This is merely one illustration of what, with many conductors, went on all through the symphony. But hope springs eternal in the human breast, and I am still optimistic enough to believe that one of these days I shall hear the Pathetic as it really is. But until I can be sure of that I shall prefer reading it to listening to it, either in the concert room or on gramophone records.

BLOCH'S 'SACRED SERVICE':

A WORK JEWISH AT HEART

3rd April 1938

On Saturday evening last there was broadcast from Birmingham the first English performance of Ernest Bloch's 'Sacred Service'. The broadcast was barbarously terminated by a fade-out some minutes before the end; but by that time listeners had had an opportunity to sample the fine quality of this work, which has always held a high place in the esteem of students of Bloch. It was written between 1932 and 1934, after the composer's return to Europe from a long residence in America; it dates, therefore, from that period of his brooding upon the present sorry condition of the world that gave birth also to the piano sonata (1935). For some reason or other both the full score and the piano score were published by an Italian firm—Carisch, of Milan. The former contains only Hebrew words; the latter has, in addition to the Hebrew, an Italian version from which it is clear that the texts employed are Old Testament ones familar to us all. (I understand that there is now an edition with English words, published by Boosey and Hawkes. Presumably this was used for the broadcast. Oddly enough, the words of the officiating minister at one point—'May the time not be distant, O God, when Thy name shall be worshipped in all the earth', etc.—though in Italian, like the rest of the Service, in the Carisch vocal score, are given in English in the full score.)

I am rather surprised to hear that there have been numerous performances of the Service in America and on the Continent, not only in the concert room but also in the synagogues. I know nothing of the synagogue, but I should have thought the Service was planned on too big a scale for performance there, calling as it does for an orchestra of thirty-five strings, full wood wind, four horns, three trumpets, three trombones, tuba, two harps, celesta, and a considerable quantity of percussion. For the rest, it requires a solo baritone (the Cantor), and a mixed choir.

The Birmingham performance was conducted by G. D. Cunningham. The Cantor's music was sung nobly and fervently by Roy Henderson. The choral part did not come over very well, perhaps because of some defect in the transmission. The work calls for a large choir with a special kind of technique. It would well repay intensive study by one of our large London Choirs, and the sooner we hear it at Queen's Hall the better, for it is a remarkable creation.

The composer has told us that while it relates primarily to the Jewish Sabbath morning service it is meant to be of universal appeal. It has to be listened to with minds from which all associations with Christian structures such as the Mass have been temporarily banished. The Catholic Mass is a skilful piece of dramatic construction, providing liberal contrasts and telling climaxes. There is nothing dramatic about the Sacred Service; this is mainly contemplative and philosophical, though of course there are high lights as well as low. For Jewish listeners the work no doubt has a communal significance at many points: but for the rest of us its interest resides mainly in the intensity of the composer's personal expression.

There are several leading motives, the one most frequently used being the short Mixolydian phrase (the scale of G to G with F natural) with which the Service opens; the simplicity of this allows of it being adapted to all kinds of purposes, harmonic, contrapuntal and rhythmic. The specifically Jewish elements in the music are comparatively rare: we meet with an occasional Oriental melisma or a harmonic complex with other fundamental associations than those of the usual modern European scale, but nowhere do these 'exoticisms' clash with the general 'Western' texture of the music. Manifestly, however, even when working along apparently traditional lines, the imagination at the back of it all is specifically Blochian; the choral writing in particular has a stamp of its own.

Universal as I believe the appeal of the work to be, it is of course Jewish at heart: Bloch may mourn the sufferings that the modern world has brought on itself by its blindness and its cruelty, but he obviously suffers in the first place as a Jew. His aspiration for a better world in which hatred and division shall have made way for human brotherhood is universal in its scope, but even for the non-Jewish listener what gives this music its peculiarly moving quality is the cry throughout it all of a sorely persecuted race.

The most tragic feature of the Service, for me, is the evident inner clash between Bloch's mind and his heart. There are many occasions on which the words say one thing and the music, it seems to me, another, as if doubt and despair were always weighing down the wings of hope. Take, by way of illustration, the unison choral cry, in the first section, of 'Hearken, O Israel; the Lord our God is One', a cry that is repeated in the third section, and again near the end of the work. Is it in accents such as these that a community expresses its sure conviction? In each case the phrase terminates in a wild orchestral dissonance: in the second instance the dissonances culminate in a heartrending orchestral cry. (The marking is *doloroso*.) The same procedure occurs after the words 'The Lord shall reign to all eternity'; not only do G's and F sharps tug against each other in the voices, but as soon as these have ceased the full orchestra gives out a tearing minor ninth as a prelude to a short interlude that is agonised from start to finish. As I have said, it is as if the composer, in his heart of hearts, had little belief in his own words of faith and hope. I know no other religious music that presents us with an intellectual and emotional dilemma of this strange kind.

The Service has to be listened to at every point in the way appropriate to itself, not in the way to which the settings of the same or similar words by Christian composers have accustomed us. The exaltation that comes of religious confidence is nowhere to be found in this work of Bloch's. Listen, for example, to Handel's setting, in the 'Messiah,' of 'Lift up your heads, O ye gates, and the King of Glory shall come in,' and then to Bloch's. There is nothing in the latter's setting of this passage of the triumphal assurance, the pictorial pageantry, of the Christian treatment of the words. Whether the musical phrases he employs are traditional to the Jewish service or not I cannot say: be that as it may, the fact remains that the dominant mood is one not of exultation, or even of exaltation, but, in some curious fashion, of difficulty to be faced. In this ritual there is no sense of victory. Recall Handel's ebullient setting of the words that follow—'Who is the King of Glory? The Lord strong and mighty, the Lord mighty in battle'—and then observe how Bloch treats them. To the question of the chorus the Cantor answers 'Adonai Sabaoth, He is the King of Glory.' The 'Adonai Sabaoth' is indeed marked *fieramente*, but there is no elaboration of that mood, which, indeed, subsides instantly into a *dolce* at the words 'He is the King of Glory': this is followed by a softly-breathed 'Selah, selah' by the choir, and this by an orchestral interlude of quiet intensity—or intense quietude—as the Scroll is taken out of the ark.

Bloch's whole treatment of the Bible texts is interesting for its complete difference from the methods we are accustomed to. The expression he puts into them is equally new: that it is largely racial as well as personal is evident from the fact that in the final pages of the work the musical idiom, which, for all its closeness of touch with traditional Jewish elements, has hitherto been that of modern music in general, now becomes more specifically racial. All in all the 'Sacred Service' is a remarkable creation, significant not only for the light it throws on Bloch as a musician but also for the light it throws on a grievously tried people. Now that sympathy for the Jews has risen to such heights in this country, a large-scale performance of the Service in London would be not merely a musical event of the first importance but a gesture of human fellowship.

BRAHMS AND THE GREEK SPIRIT

21st January 1940

JUST before the war broke out I had occasion to refer to a new book by the leading German Nietzschean, Professor Alfred Baeumler, *Studien zur deutschen Geistesgeschichte*. A few days ago I happened to be reading the letters of Hölderlin, a fine poet and singularly attractive personality, a contemporary of Goethe and Schiller, whose work is too little known to the generality of English readers. Recalling Professor Baeumler's remarks on Hölderlin in his essay on 'Hellas und Germanien' I took up his book again, and once more was mightily impressed by his confident exposition of the thesis that the modern Germans are the true heirs of Greek culture. That thesis has been a favourite one with German writers for many years: it is merely one more exemplification of that engaging modesty that compels the Germans to admit the truth about themselves, even when it appears to verge almost on flattery. One's only regret is that the ancient Greeks were not aware of the spiritual family reunion they were missing by dying more than twenty centuries too soon; for us in other and more barbarian countries, also, there would be a thrill in hearing Plato call Dr. Goebbels brother, and seeing Epicurus clasp the lilywhite hand of Herr Himmler.

While musing wistfully upon this lofty subject I discovered that from somewhere or other the B.B.C. was just about to broadcast a performance of Brahms's 'Song of Destiny'. The words of this are by Hölderlin, and good Brahmsians have always assured us that the music represents the composer's closest approach to the Greek spirit. After the performance of the 'Song of Destiny', which has long been a great favourite of mine, I read through the scores of certain others of those smaller works of Brahms for voices and orchestra that are so unaccountably neglected in England, though they contain some of his finest music. The 'Alto Rhapsody' (words by Goethe) does not concern me here; for the moment I am concerned only with the three works in which the German-'Greek' spirit finds expression in the poems—the 'Song of Destiny', the 'Song of the Fates', (words from Goethe's 'Iphigenie') and the 'Nänie' (words by Schiller).

Looking at these scores again, after the lapse of some years, I had to confess that I could no longer find in them the 'Greek' quality I had been taught to see in them. This music, if Professor Baeumler will forgive me for saying so, is mostly far too German to be very Greek: it is too thick about the waist and too heavy on its feet for that. Nor can I any longer subscribe to a dogma we all dutifully took for granted at one time—that in the final orchestral section of the 'Song of Destiny' Brahms intended to console us for the pessimism he and the poet had poured out on us in the preceding section. The reader will no doubt remember that the poem is in three stanzas, in the first two of which Hölderlin paints the felicity of the immortals in their abode of beauty and light, while the third stanza depicts the hard and irremediable lot of man on earth. Brahms reproduces the former picture in an orchestral prelude and a chorus of tranquil loveliness, and the second in a chorus of drastic harshness of expression. Then, according to the theory accepted, unable to bear the thought of leaving us in this hopeless 'pagan' mood, he consoles us—some pious writers even speak of 'Christian consolation'—with a repeat of the orchestral prelude, which brings the fine work to an exquisite end.

It is perhaps possible, however, to explain Brahms's procedure more simply, in terms not of philosophy but of rudimentary musical form. Of the three 'Greek' poems, two, the 'Schicksalslied' and the 'Gesang der Parzen', confront the musician with peculiar formal difficulties. The 'Nänie' was easy enough; the overriding uniformity of its moods enabled Brahms to round off the musical close by a simple return to the opening strain. But over the 'Gesang der Parzen' Brahms broke down completely. His setting of Goethe's fifth stanza is truly nonsensical; his suave music—his own marking for this section is 'sehr weich'—flies in the very face of the pitiless sentiment of the words. It is useless to try, as some apologists have done, to explain away this wrong procedure on pseudo-philosophical lines. The plain fact is that Brahms solved, to his own satisfaction if not ours, his problem of form here as he does more than once in his songs, arbitrarily imposing a certain procedure of musical contrast upon the words at a particular point of a poem, whether that be the most rational psychological point for such a change or not. In the case of the 'Gesang der Parzen', the quite irrational softening of the music in the stanza 'Es wenden die Herrscher' was dictated purely and simply by the feeling Brahms had that some musical variety was desirable before he wound up his work by a return to the uncompromising hardness of the opening; and he merely obeyed a general law of his subconscious self as an artist in inserting this musical variety just where he was accustomed to do, regardless of the general sense of the poem.

I feel that the repeat, as postlude, of the beautiful orchestral prelude of the 'Schicksalslied' came about purely and simply because there was nothing else open to Brahms by way of ending. The two antithetical choral sections are perfect individually, but from the point of view of musical form they are incomplete. Brahms, as we know, thought at one time of a choral ending with a repeat of the opening words of the poem. He did at once the obvious and supremely sensible thing by rounding his work off in simple A B A form by repeating the instrumental prelude. There is no need to talk, as one orthodox old-school Brahmsian does, of Brahms thus conveying to us that he 'had more confidence in a future life than the poet expressed'.

MORE ABOUT BRAHMS

28th January 1940

As I expected, my article last week on the 'Song of Destiny' and certain other choral-orchestral works of Brahms has brought me some correspondence. Most of it is concerned with the interpretation to be put upon the employment of the orchestral prelude to the 'Song of Destiny' to form the postlude.

A friend suggests that there may be another explanation of this besides the simple impulse on the composer's part to round off his work by a resort to A B A form. She asks whether 'the repetition of the lovely first theme may not be meant to symbolise the *indifference* of the gods? While poor mankind is hurtling blindly down into the abyss, *they* go on 'wandelnd droben im Licht auf weichem Boden', etc. The pagan gods, when not interfering in human affairs from the lowest and pettiest of motives, were as indifferent as Nature. And the Great Mind—God, or Fate, or Anangkē, or whatever we may call it—is as beautifully indifferent too. So there need be no inconsistency in reminding us of the happy gods. It only makes our own fate more painful by contrast.' With this I fully agree. But I submit that it constitutes a secondary problem for the primary one. If we ask ourselves what Brahms *could* have done, by way of rounding off his work musically, except just what he has done, we are compelled to reply, Nothing. The orchestral repeat was rooted in the very nature of things. That is what I call the primary problem. The secondary problem is what philosophical connotations were set up in Brahms's own mind by the repeat. In my article I was concerned only to question the validity of the traditional explanation of the repeat—that after the stark pessimism of Hölderlin's last verse Brahms wanted to administer a little 'Christian consolation' to us by repeating the serene music of the prelude. Just what Brahms thought about this matter we do not know; but for the rest of us surely the effect of the postlude is precisely that described by my friend—the repetition of the picture of the bliss of the gods does not 'correct' the pessimism of the final verse but gives an extra sadness to it.

While I am on this subject there are one or two points that call for a little more discussion than I had space for last week. I myself cannot see anything particularly 'Greek' in Brahms's music to the 'Schicksalslied', the 'Gesang der Parzen', and the 'Nänie'. I could not define very exactly what I and others have in mind when we speak of 'Greek' in this connection; and I myself would prefer to use the term 'Mediterranean', meaning by that a texture, and beyond that a spirit, woven of finer strands and vibrating with a purer, warmer light than is the general lot of man in more northern countries. I can see nothing of this in Brahms even at his most 'Greek': the texture of his mind and of his speech is still the product of a land in which the blood courses more sluggishly than in the favoured south. For expressions of this truly 'Greek' spirit, if we are going to agree to call it that, we must look elsewhere than to modern German music—to some of the music of France, or to the incomparably beautiful flute melody in the scene in the Elysian Fields in Gluck's 'Orfeo'. At the same time it has to be admitted that in the prelude and the postlude to the 'Schicksalsied' Brahms has achieved a poignancy of beauty that cannot be paralleled anywhere else in all his work. We do not need the testimony of his friends to persuade us that Hölderlin's poem moved him as few poems had ever done.

One of the reasons for the 'Schicksalslied', the 'Gesang der Parzen' and the 'Nänie' being more German than 'Greek' is that in all of them the rhythm is much more Brahms than Hölderlin, Goethe or Schiller. The choral texture of the works, of course, of itself dictates a certain metrical four-squareness of melodic phrasing, in which the characteristic rhythm of the poems is bound to disappear. But there would have been the same loss in whatever other form Brahms had chosen for his settings. For Brahms could generally be trusted to paralyse the rhythmic nerve of any poem that did not run along the simplest metrical lines. It is not a matter of neglected opportunities of right verbal accent or the sheer musical tyranny that sometimes imposes a downright wrong accent upon the poetic line, though there are some rather painful instances of this in the works we are discussing, as in many other works of Brahms. More serious than this is his complete failure, obsessed as he so often is by melodic-metrical formulae derived from German popular song, to reproduce in his music even the smallest suggestion of that subtle cross-fertilisation of sense and sound that constitutes so much of our pleasure when we read these poems. Even the reader without a close acquaintance with German poetic rhythms will see what I mean if he will get thoroughly into him the lilt of the opening lines of the 'Nanie':

Auch das Schöne muss sterben! Das Menschen und Götter
    bezwinget,
Nicht die eherne Brust rührt es des stygischen Zeus;

and then take up Brahms's score and see how he has massacred the rhythm for his own purely musical purposes.

So far as my own knowledge of the subject goes, poems couched in the German hexameter form have in general been fought shy of by German song composers. The best things I can remember in this field are the Russian Medtner's fine settings of two poems by Goethe—'Einsamkeit' and 'Geweihter Platz.' And why has Hölderlin been so strangely neglected by the German composers? Can any of my readers tell me whether his noble 'An die Parzen' has ever been attempted in music?

'WOZZECK'

I

How much longer is the remarkable 'Wozzeck' to wait for a stage production in London? That our public knows anything at all about it is due entirely to the B.B.C., which gave us a concert performance of it in Queen's Hall (that was also broadcast in the Home Service), and one in the studio, broadcast in the Third Programme.

Everything about 'Wozzeck' is amazing. To begin with, Büchner's drama. If a manuscript of this had come to light for the first time the other day and been published by the finder of it as the work of a German boy who died in 1837 in his 24th year there would have been the sharpest doubts expressed as to its authenticity. No one, it would have been contended, could thus have anticipated our modern half-mad schizophrenic world in 1836, and least of all a young German only just out of his teens.

An interesting subject for study, by the way, would be the influence of a medical training on some of the musicians and literary men of the early 19th century. Büchner, Flaubert and Berlioz, for example, were all the sons of doctors, studied anatomy, and, in some cases, 'walked the hospitals' and practised or witnessed dissection. So did one or two of the characters in Murger's 'Scènes de la vie de Bohème'; and we have evidence enough that the hospitals and dissecting rooms of that epoch were rather horrible. It is no wonder that sensitive young artists who went through these experiences developed a taste for the cynical gruesome-grotesque which it took them some time to shake off.

In Büchner's case the sense of the crazy precariousness of the balance of the human mind and body was shot with a pity for poor humanity that was none the less burning for being so objective in its expression. In his case the result of it all was a drama in which hardly one of the chief characters is quite normal; each of them is poised dizzily on a small point on the borderline between sanity and insanity. Could such a subject be re-conceived in music? Berg decided that it could; and by an astonishing concurrence of all the necessary factors, some of them personal, others made possible by the new turn that music had taken about the beginning of the present century, he managed to bring it off. No one else could have done it.

Obviously the older harmonic idiom and the older routines of opera construction would not suffice for a theme of this kind. To begin with, much of what these characters are saying could not possibly be *sung* in the ordinary way; nor could it be simply spoken. So Berg, following the lead of Schönberg, decided, for certain episodes, on the sort of 'speech melody' he defines in a foreword to his score. Though the notes are written at definite musical pitches they are not to be sung as a melody. Nor, on the other hand, are the words to be delivered in the ordinary speaking voice: there must be a compromise between the two procedures.

The result is often distressing to the musical ear, though in practice, indeed, some of the performers find their purely musical instincts and habits too strong to be overcome by any effort of the will, and they keep slipping back into the 'singing' style which Berg expressly says he does not want. But whether we wholly approve of it or not, there can be no question that Berg was right in this particular instance.

Obviously again, the established opera forms would be incongruent with such a drama as 'Wozzeck'; so Berg saw it in terms of a new form. Each of the fifteen scenes that make up the three acts is cast in one of the forms of instrumental music —sonata form, fugue, passacaglia, and so on. To all this there can be no a priori objection. The chaconne long ago proved its dramatic value in opera—witness the death song of Purcell's Dido.

But these are simple matters; to recognise the rightness of Berg's choice of a particular form for a particular situation, and to appreciate the combination of craftsmanship and dramatic imagination with which he has handled his material, necessitates much hard work at the score. A great deal of the ingenuity of it is bound to pass unnoticed by the ordinary listener. He will presumably spot without any difficulty the fugal subject and answer in the second scene of the second act, but I doubt whether he will be able to follow the whole course of the passacaglia that is the best form that could have been chosen for the expression of the *idée fixe* of the crazy Doctor in the fourth scene of the first act.

This does not mean that Berg was ever wrong in going about his technical-dramatic job the way he did: the trouble is simply that for us to see it all as he saw it involves a great deal of hard intellectual exercise. That notwithstanding this the ordinary listener feels that the music is always 'right', always the only possible move for a scene, is testimony enough to Berg's technical skill and imaginative power.

We will consider next week some other features of the work, in particular it's harmonic idiom, which is of more than one kind, but always the right kind for the character or the situation of the moment.

II

3rd April 1949

I SAID last week that everything about 'Wozzeck' is amazing, from Büchner onwards. Berg's contribution makes the work unique. There is no fear of any later opera composer following in his wake, even if that were wholly desirable; even more than is the case with 'Pelléas et Mélisande', here is something which in its totality had no forerunners and is most unlikely to have any legitimate and healthy successors.

Whether you 'like' the opera or not, and even if you jib at some of it, you have to admit that the thing, incredible as it would have appeared a priori, has come off, and that no other composer before Berg or since could have brought it off. Of all the works bearing the Schönberg seal—I mean, of course, the

Schönberg of the period that succeeded the 'Gurrelieder' and
the 'Verklärte Nacht'—this is the only one that has seized upon
the imagination of the ordinary music lover and brought him
back to the hearing of it again and again.

How has Berg managed it? Not by virtue of those 'forms',
mostly new to opera construction, on the handling of which the
analyst loves to dilate. There was no reason whatever why Berg
should not use these or any other routines of stylisation if he
felt they would further his purpose. Still, forms exist for music's
sake, not music for the form's sake. Everything depends on what
the composer has managed to do with them. Berg himself was
perhaps inclined, as Schönberg was and still is, to overvalue the
logic of musical procedure in and by and for itself. Schönberg,
we learn, used to illustrate the process of theme-transformation
in musical composition by taking a soft felt hat, stretching and
kneading and twisting it into all sorts of shapes, and then saying,
'You see, it still remains the same hat.'

But, as I think I have remarked before, all this leaves out of
the reckoning the essence of the matter—the original quality of
the material of the hat and the value of it as a piece of apparel,
in its various metamorphoses: of what avail is all the ingenuity
that has been expended on transforming it if the final product
is a hat that no one would care to be seen in in Piccadilly?

Berg too could fall into the quite academic error of supposing
that if a musical work is well made it is necessarily good music.
A moment's consideration will convince the least skilled in
music that this is a classroom or text-book fallacy. It would be
easy, for instance, to construct a symphonic first movement
that should be an exact reduplication of the construction of that
of the Eroica; but it would not, on that account, be another
Eroica. In 1924 Berg wrote an enthusiastic and exhaustive
analysis of Schönberg's D minor string quartet, op. 7 (1907).
One follows with the greatest interest his demonstration of the
constructional power shown in the quartet; but we still remain
unconvinced, in 1949, that this is a piece of music of the first
order.

No, the proof of every pudding is in the eating; and if the
eating is good the ordinary man is not very curious about the
proportions of the ingredients or the technique of the cook. So

'Wozzeck' is aesthetically neither better nor worse for its 'forms'; all that matters in the end is the quality of the music. At home one goes with pleasure through the intellectual exercise of tracing all the threads of the various patterns; but when listening to 'Wozzeck' one forgets or puts aside most of what one has learnt in this way and simply surrenders oneself to the broad musical impression. The non-technical listener, indeed, can do nothing else but this.

The thing that matters is that somehow or other, by a unique combination of craftsmanship and imagination, Berg has brought off the seemingly impossible. What looks like sheer caprice on paper, and is frankly intolerable when the reader of the score hears it mentally in terms of most of the other music to which he is accustomed—that is to say, music as a black-and-white drawing touched up in colour—sounds exactly right when heard as Berg intended it to be heard, the colour not being merely laid on a pre-existent design but constituting an integral part of the idea.

A simple illustration will serve. What could be more awful in the black-and-white of the piano or a piano score, than a downward slither of some twenty successive minor ninths? But listen to them in the ghostly pianissimo of two solo violins, with a shuddering bare fourth below them in the violas, playing tremolando on the bridge, and you can have no doubt that here is the perfect, the inevitable realisation, technical and pictorial and psychological, of the grisly horror of the scene in which the distracted Wozzeck searches in the moonlight for the knife that may lead to the tracing of Marie's murder to him.

The non-technical listener to the opera finds himself, perhaps for the first time in his life, taking in a vast amount of non-tonal music and not merely not wincing at it but being engrossed by it. That simple fact is the true measure of Berg's achievement; whether the listener can account for his interest or not the fact remains that he *is* interested in 'Wozzeck' throughout, that he feels this music to be not only 'right' for the subject but the only musical equivalent conceivable for it. Still, he feels most at home, perhaps, in the last act, of the harmonic idiom of which I will have something to say next week.

III

10th April 1949

How does the plain musical man 'hear' 'Wozzeck'; that is to say, how does he fit, or fail to fit, the sounds into the categories of his general musical experience?

We need not spend any time in discussing whether the more repellent portions of the score are or are not atonal in the strictest sense of that term. Let us agree to call them non-tonal, a word which, for practical purposes, will cover both music that discards tonality of set theoretical intention and music which, without any doctrinaire prepossessions, strays at times so far afield from tonality that the ordinary listener feels he has lost his way.

It is only by a conscious effort that the average man can think non-tonally for any stretch of time, so rooted is the tonal habit in him. To frankly atonal music he listens with the inherited tonal relationships of notes always at the back of his mind, seizing whenever he can, like a drowning man snatching at a hen-coop, upon a chord that suggests to him a tonal centre —though the composer never intended it as such—and regarding the surrounding notes simply as capricious deviations from the norm of harmonic logic. Even those of us who have put in many hours of hard work at the 'Wozzeck' score often find a difficulty, during a performance, in thinking our way through the texture, as distinct from responding to it *en masse*.

Why then does the work grip as it does even the listener without any theoretical training? I suppose it is because of the unique oneness of the dramatic situations, the psychology of the characters, and the musical expression. The first two of these elements are so consistently irrational that a certain irrationality (as the ordinary listener conceives it) in the music also seems right, especially in view of the fact upon which I dwelt last week, that what revolts our harmonic sensibility in black-and-white can be made not only tolerable but gladly acceptable by means of orchestral colour. But, once more, the acceptance of a divergence into the abnormal implies the background of norm.

Everyone knows the electrifying effect of the episode in 5/4 time in the third act of the opera in which Tristan, in his delirium, tears the bandages from his wound. Simple as the

153

device of an 'irregular' metre is, it serves its end to perfection—
that of suggesting a mind suddenly broken loose from its moor-
ings in sanity. As it happens, Handel had long ago done the
same thing in his opera 'Orlando', and thereby rather upset his
formal-minded 18th-century audiences. 'The whole last scene
of this act', said Burney, 'which paints the madness of Orlando,
in accompanied recitatives and airs in various measures, is
admirable. Handel has endeavoured to describe the hero's perturbation of intellect by fragments of symphony in 5/8, a
division of time which can only be borne in such a situation.'

In the 'Wozzeck' of 1914–20, as in the 'Orlando' of 1733 and
the 'Tristan' of 1865, the hearer cheerfully grants the composer
his little licences of harmony or rhythm in the portrayal of
'perturbation of intellect.' But just as a perturbation of intellect
is recognised as such only against a norm of intellectual stability,
so does the listener's acceptance of an 'abnormal' harmony
depend upon the general recognition of an harmonic norm in
these things.

We might sum up, perhaps, that while the non-tonal system
may have, in the present state of our harmonic development,
validity in some spheres of expression, we instinctively feel that
it is invalid in others, and Berg himself seems tacitly to admit
this in his third act, which, as it happens, always makes the
profoundest impression on the audience.

It has often been asked whether we can imagine, at any rate
just yet, an atonal Romeo and Juliet or Papageno or Desdemona.
Anyhow Berg seems to have decided that for the limning of the
poor simple humanity of his Marie a nearer approach to
tonality would be necessary than in the case of the other main
characters. Here he is obviously doing no more than carrying
a stage further the chromatic subtilisations of tonality accom-
plished by Wagner in 'Tristan' and 'Parsifal'. Often, indeed,
the music of this third act is the frankest reminiscence of actual
passages in those two works: the episode beginning at bar 323 on
page 224 of 'Wozzeck', for instance, suggests how Wagner
himself might have handled certain episodes in 'Parsifal' had
he lived another twenty years or so. 'Wozzeck' is a Janus work,
with one face turned towards the past, the other towards the
future.

'WOZZECK'

ON THE FIRST PRODUCTION IN ENGLAND

27th January 1952

As well as I could judge, 'Wozzeck' last Tuesday made just the effect on its audience that I had anticipated; whether people 'liked' it or not it got hold of them and shook them out of themselves.

There are two features of the opera that are calculated to go rather against it at first with the ordinary listener—the Sprechgesang that endures throughout the greater part of it, and the complex harmonic idiom. To innovations in both these fields Berg was inevitably pre-committed both by the nature of the dramatic subject and by the idiosyncrasies of the dramatist's style. Büchner never indulges in sentiment, and rarely lets his own emotion be seen. He goes straight to his point, makes it in the fewest words possible, and then leaves it to the reader or the spectator to supply all the emotional reaction that may be required.

There is hardly a sentence in the whole play that calls for lyrical or symphonic expansion of the traditional type. Everywhere, with the one exception to which I shall refer in a moment, the composer has perforce to aim at an objectivity that shall match Büchner's; nowhere can the musician speak to us *in propria persona*, never have the air of saying 'See how pathetic my characters are in their sufferings and their follies, how sorry I myself am for them, and how sorry I am going to make you too.' In the second place, a vocal line would have to be found that would not deflect us by age-old associations into emotional connotations of an older kind.

To take this last point first. We may as well admit that the vocal line has few amenities for the musical ear, that for the most part it is neither song nor talk, that sometimes it fails even to achieve its declared purpose of reproducing the accents and contours of ordinary speech, and that occasionally it is naively ridiculous. While all this is true, it remains equally true that for Büchner's drama and Büchner's text no other species of treatment than that given them by Berg is conceivable. He obeyed

155

a sound instinct in making the texture of his opera just what it is.

It was an experiment in a new genre, and we must not demand final perfection from pioneers; let us remember that for his new vocal line in particular he had practically no model but Schönberg's monodrama 'Erwartung', which is in itself a mere first groping in a territory uncharted until then. It may be that a couple of hundred years hence 'Wozzeck' will be looked back upon very much as we look back on some of the experiments of Monteverdi and his Italian contemporaries—as the work of a man of rare genius confronted by the double, the baffling, task of not merely building himself a new house but making his own bricks and having to solve unaided a dozen new problems of material stresses and strains.

With the orchestral tissue the plain musical man need not have over-much difficulty. Strange as it often is, it mostly makes the desired effect straight away on the non-technical listener. It goes straight to the point, and having made it, goes on at once to the next. Without ever aiming at effect for mere effect's sake it is always effective. It remains true, however, that the profoundest impression is made on the ordinary listener by the few pages in which the musical idiom avails itself gladly of the resources of the older tonality—the superb orchestral interlude before the final stage scene. This music tears one's heart out; and technically it is simply a further development of the language of 'Tristan' and 'Parsifal.'

Was the resort to this language, as some have thought, a sigh of relief on Berg's part at being able to escape for a little while from his self-imposed fetters of non-tonality and speak the traditional tongue of music as only he among his younger contemporaries had it in him to do? Or was the change of tone at this point the last and most convincing proof on his part that his general musical procedure in the opera until then had been right? For in these extraordinarily moving pages, with no words to constrain him, he does what we had all along been cherishing at least a half-hope that he would do—he drops his Büchnerian mask of detachment and pours out his own copious vials of compassion on his pitiful creatures and generous resentment at the constitution of a universe that allows such suffering. He had held all this back until the right moment—when the actual drama was virtually over; and now he releases a flood of feeling that had long been pent up not only in him but in us.

Kleiber's handling of the performance was, as might have been expected, masterly. The production was in general good, though sometimes more naturalistic than eerie. Of the very capable cast, Marko Rothmüller made the greatest impression with a remarkable Wozzeck. The opera was sung in an English translation by Vida Harford and Eric Blackall. They have done their difficult job extremely well, though one felt at times that the English tongue does not take kindly to the German Sprechgesang.

'WOZZECK'

THIS 'SPRECHGESANG'

10th February 1952

I SEEM to have devoted a good deal of my space to 'Wozzeck' lately, but the importance and the novelty (for this country) of the work have necessitated it. But one feature of the opera has had to go undiscussed—the vocal line, or at any rate so much of that line as comes under the definition of Sprechgesang. The music-lover who intends to listen to the end to the broadcasts the B.B.C. is now giving us of Schönberg's music will have to concern himself a good deal, willy-nilly, with that curious modern product. But 'Wozzeck' must already be giving the plain musical man much to think about and to make him a trifle uncomfortable; and perhaps it is as well for him to try to take his bearings in the Sprechgesang now, while Berg's opera is still accessible to him at Covent Garden.

The word has hitherto meant for him simply a dodge, a fake, by which certain Wagnerian singers who couldn't sing used to *speak* their notes at (approximately) the pitches noted in the score. But that is not what the term means today in the school that has stemmed from Schönberg. The Wagnerian Sprechgesang—sometimes referred to irreverently in days of old as 'the Bayreuth bark'—pretended to be what it wasn't, namely, bel canto at a certain remove. The modern Sprechgesang is not a pretence, a fake designed to get a poor technician over a vocal difficulty, but a form of expression used seriously for its own sake. What, then, is it essentially?

If the reader looks up 'Sprechgesang' in his German dictionary he will find it defined as 'recitative'. But his ears tell him that it is decidedly not recitative in the sense he ordinarily attaches to that word, the sense it carries, for instance, in 'Don Giovanni' or 'Messiah', where a portion of the text not calling for or lending itself to formal lyrical outpouring is given the accents, the contours, the pace, the free arhythmic flow of speech but remains, for all that, *music*, tied to definite note-pitches demanding to be *sung*.

Now for the performer or the listener to hear 'Wozzeck' just as the composer intended it to be performed or listened to he must approach the vocal line from the correct angle. At present many people appear to be going slightly astray. I have noticed an increasing tendency on the part of some of the singers to *sing* this 'Sprechgesang' passage or that; it is what they would naturally do, for they have been trained as singers, they regard it as their primary duty to sing, and the sight of words set to notes of definite pitches in the stave almost irresistibly lures them into singing the phrase in the way to which their ordinary musical practice has accustomed them. But this is quite wrong in cases such as those we are now considering.

When the singer *sings* this music in the ordinary way he decoys the listener also into conceiving it as melody of the ordinary kind; and as such it probably has little to commend it to his musical ear. Hence, I think, the rage of some correspondents who have written to tell me how they hate this 'so-called music.' They have been listening in the wrong way; not having been given what their 'musical ear' had been expecting, they are disappointed and angry. I don't say whether they are justified or unjustified in this. I merely state a fact, and at the conclusion of the B.B.C. Schönberg broadcasts an opportunity may arise for a more thorough discussion of the problem in all its bearings.

Meanwhile, as regards 'Wozzeck', the listener should make himself acquainted with the explanation Berg has given of his procedures in a prefatory note to the score, which follows, for the most part, Schönberg's preface to his 'Pierrot Lunaire.' There are really three forms employed in 'Wozzeck', (1) plain everyday speech, (2) near-lyricism, (3) Sprechgesang proper: in this last, though the notes are written at definite pitches in the score, they are not to be *sung* in the ordinary way; they are to be speech—*yet not realistic-natural speech*—at approximately the musical pitches indicated in the stave. And both Berg and Schönberg lay it down emphatically that 'the performer must take particular care not to drop into a 'singing' speech-style: that is absolutely *not* what the composer intends.'

So now the singer knows what to do, and the listener what to expect or not to expect. Or do they?

MUSIC AND WORDS

23rd March 1952

THE B.B.C. is doing us a great service just now by its broadcasts of a comprehensive selection from the works of Schönberg. Of all the works of the 'real' Schönberg that might have established themselves by now in our general musical life, the 'Pierrot Lunaire', which was broadcast a few evenings ago, should have stood the best chance, if only because of the small instrumental force it calls for; but after the performance I found myself asking once more whether that interesting work has still made, or is likely to make, any real progress with the general public.

I feel, as I have always done, that what stands, and, I fear, always will stand, in the way of its acceptance is the voice part. I myself, try as I will, cannot get reconciled to this 'speaking to the note', which, as the composer says in his preface to the score, must be neither true 'speaking' nor true 'singing', nor even 'speaking' at the definite pitches indicated in the score, for 'it must never suggest to us song.' The definition, it will be seen, is richer in negative than in positive guidance.

Is the problem posed by Schönberg really insoluble in practice as distinguished from theory? Anyhow he and some of his followers have done us a service by making us uncomfortably conscious that there *is* a problem—not a new one, however, but a very old one now assuming a new form. We are up against the eternal question of whether those two inveterate enemies, words and music, can make up their quarrel once and for all, or whether the nearest they can get to a peace treaty is to agree reluctantly on certain mutual accommodations. In the lyric and in opera these accommodations have been roughly successful and acceptable: music says to words, 'You see, you need my assistance to raise you to your highest emotional potency', while words come back with 'No doubt, but please don't forget that without my clearer definition of what you are saying in your indefinite language of sound a good deal of it would lack ideal intelligibility, or even an adequate *raison d'être*.'

This more or less grudging agreement, then, works very well up to a certain point. The trouble begins when the composer wishes to avail himself of an extended text that will provide him with all the 'definition' he wants without his being under the necessity of creating a vast musical form that will both embrace the poem in its totality and allow full scope for the expression of vital detail. It was for this reason that 'melodrama' arose—the simple speaking of a long text to an illustrative instrumental accompaniment. This method was already cultivated in the eighteenth century; and I suggest that the B.B.C. might do us a good turn some evening by broadcasting a performance of Georg Benda's 'Ariadne auf Naxos' (1775). In my young days the late Stanley Hawley issued a series of works to which he gave the title of 'recitation music'—for voice and piano —which also I would commend to the attention of the B.B.C. Schumann made some experiments in this genre, as Strauss (in his 'Enoch Arden') and Grieg (in his 'Bergliot') have done in our own day.

The basic problem of all works of this sort, however, and their bearing on that now confronting us in Schönberg and elsewhere, I must leave for discussion in a further article. Here I want to say a word about a significant feature of one of the most notable of all melodramas, that in the dungeon scene in 'Fidelio', where Leonora and the jailer are digging the grave intended for the prisoner who is Florestan. This is really the nodal point of the opera, the episode in which the dramatic tension reaches its highest point before the coming of the moment of relief. Now Beethoven does not attempt to gather all the dramatic constituents of the heartrending scene into his *musical* net, for the reason among others, no doubt, that this would have meant a good deal of formal elaboration, whereas he wants to concentrate the horror as much as possible. So he finishes with formal music for the time being and resorts to melodrama, as he calls it—simple everyday speech by Leonora and Rocco, with an occasional expressive 'pointing' in the orchestra.

We are thus confronted with a paradox of aesthetic. The accepted view of the words-and-music matter is that 'music steps in when words have reached the limit of their potency' (which is somewhat comically counterbalanced by the Wagnerian theory, à propos of the Ninth Symphony, that in the finale of that work Beethoven had to resort to words because music unassisted could not take the last great step that was needed). But in the 'Fidelio' case it is pure speech—not even sung words!—that steps in when apparently, in Beethoven's opinion, music has reached the limit of its own power! Wagner, faced with the dungeon scene, would have said, 'Now is the time for me to call on music to show what it can do when the dramatic tension has reached its maximum.' Beethoven gives up the musical struggle and asks for—and receives in full measure—all the help that naked speech can give him. Can we now profit in opera by his example?

PART IV

GENERAL ARTICLES

DISCORD AND REASON

6th October 1929

I HAVE been favoured lately with a large amount of correspondence—growing, for the most part, out of some wireless talks—on the subject of modern harmony. A general agreement on this complicated question is impossible, if only because different people approach it with different backgrounds of harmonic experience; those of us whose business it is to keep abreast of current music are not in the least startled or estranged by chords that may represent the last word in horror to people who still think in terms of the half-dozen basic chords and their simpler modifications that formed the foundation of music until a few years ago. There may, of course, be a danger to us in this very familiarity with dissonance. In a phrase that seems to have caught the fancy of many of my correspondents, I hinted that we professional students and listeners may possibly be in a condition corresponding to that of the boxer who has been hammered so hard that he has ceased even to know that he is being hurt. The technical term for this condition is 'punch-drunk'; and it is not at all improbable that a prolonged course of listening to dissonance may make a man dissonance-drunk, so that he loses something of his former sensitiveness to good and bad in harmony. It is a point that has to be taken into consideration.

But putting this aside as a subject too big for cursory treatment here, it will be found, I think, that the real source of the difference of reaction of the professional and the layman to some modern works is the fact that the former, through long experience of modern harmony, sees, or fancies he sees, the idea that is at the back of the harmony and is its justification, while the latter, unable to perceive the logic of the construction, necessarily misses the connection of ideas. The whole point, then, is whether, given familiarity on the hearer's part with the language, the composer has really had something to say that was worth saying and whether he has said it clearly and in the best imaginable terms. And there can be little doubt that a good deal of modern music fails to pass this simple test.

We may take as axiomatic that if the dissonance is an organic part of the idea, the physical ear will not jib at any combination of sounds, however unrelated they may look on paper, while conversely quite a simple dissonance may irritate us if there seems to be no good reason for it in the musical thought. We had many illustrations of this truth the other evening when Strauss's 'Don Quixote' and Arthur Bliss's 'Hymn to Apollo' were given at the same Promenade concert. The Straussian dissonances were accepted by the seasoned listener not only without protest but with aesthetic joy, because they were the natural correlatives of the idea, and the idea itself was a good one; whereas some of Mr. Bliss's dissonances were obviously only plastered upon a texture and an idea that were proceeding placidly along on quite another plane until the composer suddenly remembered that he must do something to show that he is a post-war modern. It was not that these particular dissonances were at all extravagant. As a matter of fact they were quite harmless; the only trouble with them was that they did not convince us of the musical necessity of their coming just when and where they did. The phenomenon of harmonic pungency for pungency's sake is not, as some people think, a new one. It already existed in the middle of the nineteenth century; and Liszt hit off the situation for all time in the remark that 'cigar ash and sawdust steeped in aqua fortis do not make pleasant soup.'

There is nothing new under the sun; and what is happening today was long ago analysed by an old gentleman named Richard Wagner, who not only wrote very good music of his own but indulged in some hard thinking about the art. In one of his later essays he pointed out that the operatic composer can permit himself a much wider range of harmony and modulation than the purely instrumental composer can, because in the former case the cause and the justification of a seeming extravagance are made apparent to the listener by the words or the stage action, while in the latter case the departure from the norm has to justify itself by the inner logic of the musical line. Let us apply this simple principle to some recent music. Here is a quotation from one of Stravinsky's Three Pieces for String Quartet:

(The reader must conceive the passage in terms of the strings; the effect on the piano is very different. The topmost part is played by the viola, and there is a crescendo between the first and second notes of each group, with a sforzando on the second.)

Here is a passage from 'Petrouchka' that obviously comes from fundamentally much the same frame of mind:

The first passage seems to me, as a piece of 'pure' music, meaningless: the second is an eloquent description of the state of mind of poor little Petrouchka, very much perturbed about things in general and fretted by the hopelessness of his love for the ballerina. In the one case the discords do not talk sense purely and simply as music; in the other case they do talk sense in view of the character and the situation.

Or take again the passage in Strauss that depicts the brain of Don Quixote cracking under the strain of impending madness —a series of discords that were rather startling when we first heard them some twenty years ago, and even today arrest the hearer's attention:

(The quotation shows only the essentials of the harmony; the reader must figure to himself, in addition, a fortissimo A natural and B flat tearing their way through the tissue in the trumpets and trombones.) Wagner was quite right: a passage of this kind would probably seem unmotived in a symphony, whereas it talks the soundest sense in a work the poetic clue to which has already been given to the listener. Moreover, although the discords themselves are physically mild in comparison with some of those of today, the passage still conveys the sensation of an intolerable strain. Why? Because there is not merely dissonance but an idea at the back of the dissonance, an idea that has preserved its vitality through the many changes in the world's musical consciousness during the last twenty years. Some of the dissonances in Mr. Bliss's work, on the other hand, already sound old-fashioned, because there is nothing in the nature of the musical thinking that confers vitality on them.

The simple truth is that our aesthetic has fallen into hopeless confusion of late. A certain school has tried to foist on us the mountebank doctrine that music must not attempt to 'express anything beyond itself'—as if the musical faculty worked in a sort of vacuum, without any infiltration into it from the outer world or from the literature that is the expression of man's experience of the world! It really will not do. There are things that can be said quite coherently and intelligibly in instrumental music alone, and there are other things that become coherent and intelligible only when the clue to them is given by words or by a stage action; and a great part of the incoherence and unintelligibility of some recent music is due to the composers of purely instrumental music having forgotten this elementary distinction.

THE COMPOSER AS 'THIEF'

5th June 1932

We had a charming example the other day of the tiny seed from which a musical legend may grow. A journalist told us, on the high authority of a tenor, how Toscanini one day sat down at the piano and showed a friend how Wagner 'used the same chords to express the word 'mother' in all his operas, from 'Rienzi' to 'Parsifal'.' So far as I remember, the word 'mother' does not occur once in 'Rienzi'; nor in 'The Flying Dutchman'; nor in 'Tannhäuser'; nor in 'Lohengrin'; nor in the 'Rhinegold'; nor in the 'Meistersinger.' It may be that I have overlooked an instance or two; but at the moment I do not think so. Toscanini, therefore, could hardly have done what he is alleged to have done. I can see, however, this legend going round the musical world for years to come.

Rousseau tells us how the scientific world in the eighteenth century was shaken to its foundations by the discovery that a boy in Silesia had been born with a golden tooth. Learned books were written about the phenomenon; papers were read before learned societies. At last it occurred to someone or other, more sceptical than the rest, to go to the village in Silesia that was said to have been the scene of this experiment, on Nature's part, in auriferous dentition; whereupon it was found that the boy's teeth were all composed of the usual substance. But I am sure the legend was believed for many years after that in France. And so it will be with this story of Wagner and the 'mother' chords.

Precisely what Toscanini really did on that occasion I do not know; but presumably he was demonstrating a characteristic of musical psychology to which I have more than once drawn attention in these columns—the practical certainty that whenever a composer happens to be in a particular mood, he will unconsciously revert to a formula which, for him, is the basic expression for that mood. This is not quite the same thing as thematic coincidence; in hundreds of instances that could be

169

cited the melodies are externally so different that their con-
sanguinity has never been suspected. It is only when we have
isolated the basic formula that we discover that hundreds of
phrases apparently quite dissimiliar can all be resolved back
into it.

There has been a good deal of not very intelligent talk about
the 'borrowings' of one composer from another, on the strength
of a similarity of melodic outline between a phrase in one and
a phrase in another. The coincidence-hunters and the would-be
restorers of stolen property have not seen that, from the very
constitution of the musical scale, different composers will often
write virtually the same succession of notes for quite different
reasons. Mendelssohn is accused of having echoed, in the phrase
marked A in the following quotation (taken from the Scotch
Symphony), a phrase (B) from the Eroica, and Wagner, in turn,
(C), of having derived a melody in the Prelude to the third
act of 'Lohengrin' from either Beethoven or Mendelssohn,
or both. But this is a very common sequence of notes, such as
might occur to any composer with the chord of the dominant
seventh in the forefront of his mind: Sullivan, for instance,
employs it in 'Patience' to express one of the woes of poor Jane
(D):—

Stout·er   than   I   used   to   be!

Commentators who have disliked Wagner have been at great
pains to demonstrate, as they imagine, that he stole most of his
themes from other composers; even Berlioz was foolish enough to
say that the theme of the Wedding Chorus in 'Lohengrin' was
lifted from Boïeldieu's 'Les Deux Nuits'—on the strength of a
chord and an accent that are the commonest small change of

music! We are solemnly asked to believe, even, that in a certain substitution of quaver-crotchet for crotchet-quaver, in itself as abundant in music as the sand on the sea-shore, this same work of Boïeldieu's, of which Wagner had probably never heard, is to be found the inspiration for a well-known passage in 'Tristan'! The people who tell us that Wagner stole his 'Treaty' motive (in the 'Ring') from Liszt's piano sonata have not gone into this grave matter deeply enough: had they probed a little further, they would have discovered that, on their own theory of 'theft', Liszt himself must have stolen the theme from the overture to Cherubini, 'Water-Carrier.' And everyone knows the similarity—quite superficial and utterly misleading, as I shall show later—between a theme in the 'Merry Wives of Windsor' overture and a passage in the 'Meistersinger'; another instance, of course, of Wagner's thievings! But just as the theory of the Baconian cypher in Shakespeare can be reduced to absurdity by the demonstration of half a dozen other cyphers, so the theory of Wagnerian borrowings can be reduced to an absurdity by pointing out coincidences in the case of other composers in which there cannot be any question whatsoever of borrowing. It is extremely improbable, for instance, that either Wagner or Johann Strauss had ever heard even the title of Boeïldieu's 'Les Deux Nuits.' Yet the following passage from that work (No. 2, A):

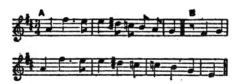

which has been solemnly described as exhibiting a 'sudden harmonic darkening that presages from afar the sententious style of Wagner', appears also (No. 2, B) in the 'Zigeunerbaron.'

One might go on in this strain ad infinitum: the resemblances are all true, and to dwell upon them is all arrant foolishness. Composers do not borrow or steal from each other like this; what they really do is much more interesting and more curious —they steal from themselves, in utter unconsciousness that they are so doing. If, a hundred times in the course of their lives, they

are faced with the same problem of expression, they will almost
certainly use, all hundred times, what I have called the same
basic formula. In the 'Blue Danube' Waltz there is a little
melodic curve which the superficial reminiscence-hunter would
say has been echoed by Richard Strauss in a love-theme of his
'Don Juan.' But when you look into the matter you see that this
curve is rooted, as it were, in Richard's psychic protoplasm;
for him it answers to a mood of high ecstasy. The 'Don Juan'
phrase is given as A of the next quotation. By its side I place
two other Strauss themes, transposed, for the convenience of
the reader, into the same key as A: B is the ecstatic cry of
Sophie when she first sees Octavian; C expresses the erotic
madness of Salome as she thinks of the forbidden lips of the
Baptist.

I propose to devote my next article or two to further examples
of self-borrowings on the part of Beethoven and of Wagner, and
perhaps, if there is space, of other composers; and, incidentally,
to give the true explanation of the alleged thefts of Wagner
from Liszt and Nicolai. It will then be seen that the so-called
Liszt and Nicolai reminiscences are merely modifications of
basic formulae that are part and parcel of Wagner's way of
musical thinking *qua* Wagner.

THE COMPOSER AS SELF-'THIEF'

12th June 1932

To show the absurdity of the 'reminiscence'-hunting that looks merely at the pitches of the notes, without taking into consideration the really vital thing, the idea of which the notes are merely the outward symbol, let us examine the case of Nicolai and Wagner.

No. 1 A shows the passage in the 'Merry Wives of Windsor' overture from which, it is alleged, Wagner derived a passage (B) in the third act of the 'Meistersinger'.

No. 1

The feature common to them both is the succession of intervals of the fourth. Now this interval happens to be characteristic of a good deal of the music in the scene in the 'Meistersinger' with which we are dealing; C and D show other phases of it. Before I go any further, however, I must forestall a certain type of criticism of the thesis I am about to put forward. When, some years ago, I cited an ascending figure of three adjacent notes as being a finger-print of Beethoven, learned reviewers all over the world pointed out that three ascending notes were to be found in many other composers! One well-informed gentleman discovered them in a song by Mozart; another, even more erudite, found them in the melody of 'Tipperary'! I did not know which to admire most, the profundity of musical knowledge that enabled these gifted publicists to quote examples from various composers in which the notes C,D,E, let us say, followed each other in that order, or the innocence that allowed them to suppose that I myself, when discussing this finger-print of Beethoven, was ignorant of the fact that these same notes appear some five hundred million times, at a moderate estimate, in the music of the last four hundred years.

As there are only twelve notes in the musical scale, it goes without saying that there is no succession of three or four of them that will not be found somewhere or other in the music of every composer who has ever lived. But the succession only constitutes a finger-print when it is unconsciously used again and again by a particular composer as the expression of what is fundamentally the same personal mood. The three-note sequence to which I drew attention is a Beethoven finger-print because it recurs time after time at virtually the same point in the phrase in dozens of his compositions, and always with the same intention, explicit or implicit.

Now intervals of the fourth are as common in melodies as any other intervals; and indeed they will be found in thousands of other places in the 'Meistersinger' than those to which I have directed the reader's attention. But examples such as those I have quoted constitute a special, though of course quite unconscious, use of fourths on Wagner's part. Used in this particular way, they are the symbol of a mood of resolution, of energy, of a decision taken, of emphatic insistence upon a point, of dignified or heavy movement. It is difficult to express a purely musical idea in a word or two, but the reader will see that basically all the moods I have mentioned have something in common; and the examples given on page 175 will perhaps make the matter clearer to him.

A is the figure of fourths used so largely in 'Parsifal' to express the stately tread of the Knights of the Grail. (In the guide-books it is called the 'Bells' motive, but this is an error. Wagner does indeed find it convenient to give the figure to the bells, but from evidence supplied by his works as a whole it becomes clear that primarily these fourths are motivated by the idea of a procession.) B is the melody to which Siegfried and Brynhilde sing the final words of their duet. 'She [he] is for ever, is for aye, my wealth and world'; here Wagner instinctively drops into

No. 2

fourths to suggest the maximum of energy and joyous resolution. C is a particularly instructive example from the end of the Kaisermarsch; after a good deal of previous insistence on fourths, Wagner hammers away at them repeatedly at the finish in order to get the maximum of emphasis into his melody. The similarity between this and B is evident at first sight.

D is rather more subtle: it is sung by Kundry to the words 'Let me upon his breast lie weeping', and repeated in various forms during the following dozen bars or so; and the melody stamps itself out in fourths because Wagner, having to express here the despair and self-reproach of Kundry at their maximum, unconsciously reverts to the formula that, for him, is inextricably interwoven with all moods expressive of a great decision taken.

E is the figure used quasi-symphonically in the first act of 'Siegfried' to symbolise the young Siegfried's physical joy in life; once more the fourths come up in Wagner's mind when he has to express a sort of stamping energy. (The reader will remember also, in this connection, the stamping fourths in the motive of the Giants.) F is a motive which the commentators have never been able to label quite satisfactorily. I lack space to discuss it in full here, but I suggest that the clue to its psychic origin may perhaps be found in its fourths, and I leave the reader to work out the problem for himself.

175

It will be seen, then, that there is not the slightest necessity to look to the 'Merry Wives' overture for the source of No. 1B: the governing interval of the fourth was virtually predestined for Wagner when he had to describe Sach's mood at this point. Moreover, in Nicolai the fourths suggest light-heartedness; whereas in Wagner a melodic sequence of that kind invariably carries quite another suggestion.

This kind of 'physiology of the composer' is not only curious and interesting in itself, but enables us to solve many a problem not only of 'plagiarism' but of style, of intention, and consequently of interpretation, especially in the case of Mozart and other old composers. In the present case it enables us to settle a little point in connection with the Siegfried Idyll. The books are wrong when they say that the motives of this are drawn from 'Siegfried'. The first main theme (bar 30 of the Idyll) was, as we now know, conceived first of all for a string quartet for Cosima, and then, years later, inserted, and that rather clumsily, in the third act of the opera. From internal evidence I suspect that the second main theme of the Idyll (bar 148, etc.) was also taken from this never-completed quartet, and adapted, still more awkwardly, to the words 'Saw'st thou thy face in the crystal brook?' But a later theme in the Idyll—that quoted as No. 2B above—was certainly written first for the opera and then transplanted to the Idyll; for with all the other evidence we have as to Wagner's fourths as a musical finger-print, we can say positively that *this* motive grew straight out of the situation and the words in the opera.

COINCIDENCES AND FINGER-PRINTS

19th June 1932

I MUST bring this series of articles to an end. Apart from the illimitability of the main subject of them, so many subsidiary points are raised by correspondents that I can see myself devoting this column to nothing else for the remainder of my days, if I live that long. Accordingly, in this final article, I deal with one or two queries which have been put to me, and touch on a typical specimen or two of Beethoven's borrowings from himself.

The downward scale used in the 'Ring' in connection with Wotan and the 'Treaty' symbol is often alleged to have been taken from Liszt's piano sonata; and a good-humoured remark of Wagner's at a rehearsal is quoted in support of that contention. But in the first place the dates are against it. The sonata was conceived between 1852 and 1853, and published in 1854. Wagner heard it first in April, 1855, when Klindworth played it to him in London. But the 'Rhinegold', in which the 'Treaty' motive occurs, was finished in January, 1854. (Wagner sent the manuscript to Liszt in September of that year; but to suppose that the sonata is in any way indebted to Wagner is as absurd as to suppose that the 'Rhinegold' was influenced by the sonata.) In the second place, this downward scale happens to be a finger-print of Wagner; it is the outward symbol, with him, of a stride. Once more let me plead the difficulty of re-phrasing music, or re-expressing a musical mood, in mere words. But it is evident that Wagner sees Wotan as a figure of vast energy, cutting his way ruthlessly through beings and circumstances in order to realise his end; and this long scale-stride is the symbol of this. We get essentially the same figure again in what is called the motive of Elisabeth's Joy at the end of the first act of 'Tannhäuser', and again in the orchestral accompaniment to her Greeting to the Hall of Song in the second act; the phrase has been unconsciously determined by the composer's vision of Elisabeth striding joyously into the Hall from which she has been absent so long—as the reader will see for himself if he will note, at the next intelligent performance he sees of the opera, the perfect congruity between the line of this phrase and the movements of Elisabeth.

By a species of psychological extension that is frequent enough in connection with musical moods, this same progression can symbolise, for Wagner, any mood of which the essence is steady continuance towards a given point. The opening phrase of the Prelude to the third act of the 'Meistersinger' shows the same down-scale line, but in a broken form. The psychological principle is basically the same as in the other cases—Sachs's brooding carries him on from point to point. (The phrase has already been used as a counterpoint to the cobbling song in the second act; but its genesis is to be sought elsewhere.) A downward scale of an octave in the introduction to Wagner's setting of Goethe's Song of the Rat (1832) may also be cited as evidence that this kind of progression was one to which Wagner was rather prone. All in all, there seems no reason to drag in Liszt for the paternity of the Wotan theme.

A song of Liszt—'Ich möchte hingehn', written some time in the 1840's, contains a bar that is curiously anticipatory of a typical 'Tristan' harmony. ('Tristan' was begun about 1857.) But there is not the slightest evidence that Wagner ever knew this song, which was not published until 1859. Moreover, to any musician it is an utterly nonsensical thesis that this single bar, which has no relation to anything else in the song, could have been fastened upon by Wagner, who promptly proceeded to evolve 'Tristan' from it! As a matter of fact, the 'Tristan' harmony is already foreshadowed in the duet between Siegmund and Sieglinde in the first act of the 'Valkyrie' (1854). The upward yearning of a couple of bars at one point in 'Ich möchte hingehn' is supposed, by some reminiscence hunters, to have given Wagner the idea of a similar passage in 'Tristan'. Unfortunately for this theory however the same phrase occurs in Wagner's Faust Overture of February 1840.

I have dealt with these various points only because, in the first place, correspondents have written me with regard to them, and in the second place to show the gross absurdity of mere reminiscence hunting. Thematic coincidences of this sort could be cited by the million, and they mean nothing at all—neither plagiarism not unconscious memory. I am surprised that some wiseacre or other has not told us before now that Wagner stole a passage in Siegfried's Rhine Journey:

from Handel's A Major violin sonata:

I will now give a few illustrations, from Beethoven, of how a composer tends to do the same thing again and again when in the same mood. Here is the opening of the slow movement of the 'Pathetic' sonata:

The controlling essence of it is the movement of the harmonic base from the tonic to the subdominant, then to the third, then to the leading note, then to the tonic, while the melody gradually rises to a climax. The same procedure is seen in the theme of the adagio of the Ninth Symphony:

In the next example, from the Coriolan overture, I skeletonise the relations of the melody and the harmony for the benefit of the reader with the minimum of technical knowledge:

The adagio of the third piano sonata shows the *tic* in a slightly different form, the principle, however, remaining the same:

The scene 'Ah perfido' shows a melodic elongation of it:

These are the merest hints of the way in which a composer unconsciously borrows from himself. From Beethoven alone I could cite examples by the thousand; a great deal of his work can easily be shown to be a series of variations upon some ten or twelve protoplasmic cell-formulae; and the same holds good of all other composers.

A WODEHOUSE STORY

AND SOME REFLECTIONS

29th March 1931

Two seemingly unrelated experiences of mine of the past week became fused into one, and then threw out a conclusion of their own, which I will put before the reader for his consideration.

On Sunday evening I tuned in to Milan and found myself listening to an opera that was completely unknown to me. I could make nothing of it musically—not that the strains in themselves confronted me with any fresh problems, for they were simplicity itself, but that they succeeded each other in so fragmentary a form that I could not pin any half-dozen of them together and make reason of them. The composer seemed to be merely illustrating this point or that in the action, and, having launched his orchestral description of the point of the moment, to be letting it go at that, leaving the words to continue the story, and waiting for the next opportunity for another fragment of orchestral illustration. The whole form was quite new to me, and in the absence of a stage representation to throw the necessary light on all these musical divagations I was very puzzled about it all. From the announcement at the end of the performance I discovered that the work was Wolf-Ferrari's new opera, a setting of Goldoni's sparkling comedy 'La vedova scaltra.'

Earlier in the same day, confronted with the choice between the Matthew Passion from Queen's Hall and Mr. P. G. Wodehouse's new novel, I had chosen the latter; for I was in the depths of misery with influenza, and for a man in that state there can hardly be any doubt that Mr. Wodehouse's medicine is a far, far better thing than Bach's. As I read on, I reflected how easy it would be for academic criticism to tear Mr. Wodehouse to pieces, and what an ass academic criticism would make of itself in the process. What academic criticism would call Mr. Wodehouse's faults are really his virtues; they may be

limitations in a sense, but only a man of genius could turn his
limitations to such splendid use. We have only to read Mr. Wodehouse *en masse* to realise the full force of Goethe's dictum that it
is in limitation that the Master reveals himself. Mr. Wodehouse
either cannot or will not invent new characters or new plots: in
his latest book we have the usual dyspeptic American million-
aire, the usual charming daughter or niece of the said million-
aire, the usual die-hard old earl with the usual Woosterish son,
the usual efficient and masterful sister of the earl, standing in
the usual relation to the usual nephew, the usual young hero
who obviously has the minimum of intelligence yet as obviously
is no fool, the usual brazen dénouement, and very much the
usual comic incidents.

Mr. Wodehouse's strength is not in invention but in treatment, which accounts for the fact that though we have met with
all these people twenty times before in his novels we are still not
yet tired of them, and will not be tired of them so long as Mr.
Wodehouse can keep it up, though we should meet with them
twenty times more. It accounts for the further fact that we can
always re-read with gusto the old Wodehouse books, while
nothing on earth would induce us to re-read the yester-year
novels of Mr. X or Mr. Z, though these gentlemen present us
with a different set of characters and a different plot and a
different series of actions in each of their books.

Mr. Wodehouse, in truth, is the last perfect representative of
a once great race of artists—the practitioners of the commedia
dell' arte. These people did not trouble about anything so easy
as inventing new forms, new settings, new characters. They took
the standardised characters of Pulcinella, Scaramouche,
Harlequin, the Captain, the Doctor, the Notary, and so on, and
recreated them afresh each time out of the abundance of their
own genius. This was really a much harder thing to do than
to invent quasi-new beings with new names, and place them in
new situations. To do that is to play a game the rules of which
you make yourself as you go along. But in the other case the
rules of the game are already agreed upon between the actors
and their audience, so that the former had either to play the
game with a new brilliance each time or be frankly given the
bird by a disappointed audience.

Something of the same state of affairs held good in the older Italian opera. Neither the composer nor his audience cared a rap, broadly speaking, for new plots, new characters, or new forms: the audience was not merely content to see, in opera after opera, the same Orfeo and Euridice, the same Titus, the same Alexander, the same Cato, the same Vitellius, the same Artaxerxes, and so on, but it was content to listen again and again to the same words, for the same text by Metastasio or some other librettist of the day would be set again and again by different composers. It is evident that under such a scheme the composer had either to get on or get out. He could not bluff his listeners into supposing that his characters were saying something musically new and individual merely because they bore new names and went through new actions: the audience took the old characters and names and actions for granted, and then insisted that the composer's job was to do with them something that none of his rivals had been able to do.

I wonder whether, one of these days, the Spirit of Music will decide to try the old method once more. The present system is one that makes for the maximum of bogus variety in externals and the minimum of actual variety in essentials. Our modern composers make it a point of honour that they shall never, so far as externals are concerned, do the same thing twice: they will omit the violins from this work and the clarinets from that: they will use the piano this time not as a solo instrument but as a constituent of the orchestra; they insist that the form of the work shall grow out of the nature and the substance of it: they are for ever seeking, as this case of Wolf-Ferrari shows, for a way of doing things that no one else has hit upon before. Yet in spite of all these changes in externals, the vital essence of their music remains monotonously the same.

What if one of these days the Spirit of Music should suddenly make up its mind that it has had enough of all this, and revert to the system of the past? What if it should decide that the licence of the musical individual has resulted in nothing but anarchy, and once more establish a *type* for each genre? I am not asserting that it will: I am only suggesting it as a possibility. But if ever that does happen, the composers, I fancy, will not find the production of music such an easy thing as it has become

now. The composer will either have to deliver the musical goods
or shut up shop. He will no longer be able to take refuge in the
magnificent logic of his theory, or lean for support upon his
collaborator the poet. The older composers needed no props
of this sort: they knew that their business, as musicians, was
simply to write music, and so they just got on with it. The
modern composer ransacks the anthologies for the finest poems.
The older composer took any old collection of words that lay
ready to his hand, and, as I have said, just got on with it.

Handel, for instance, finds in the libretto of 'Serse' some half-
dozen words that merely say, when Xerxes stands beneath a
plane tree, ' Nothing in the whole of vegetable nature makes so
agreeable a shade as this.'

There does not seem to be much in this to inspire a composer; but somehow or other Handel manages to find music
for it that makes 'Ombra mai fù' immortal. He did not disdain
the trite words as being beneath his musical dignity: he did
not sit down and worry over the discovery of a vocabulary and
a form that should be like no one else's vocabulary and form.
He just got on with it, and we all know the result. And the
result was what is was because Handel was what he was. Perhaps
the real test of the composers of the future will be when, by a
process of sheer exhaustion on everyone's part, music will
once more have reached the stage when a composer will
be judged not by his theories and his intentions but by the sort
of music he succeeds in delivering. I sometimes wonder whether
what is wrong with modern music may not be just this—that
composers are putting more brains into their job than it really
needs: too much brains and too little music.

RACIAL THEORIES AND MUSIC

WHITHER IS GERMANY TENDING?

20th March 1938

WITH politics as such, of course, I have nothing to do in this column. But politics sometimes have a close connection with questions of art; and musicians cannot help speculating as to what the recent absorption of Austria by Germany may ultimately mean for music.

It is evident at once that henceforth Austria will have to go the same way as Nazi Germany in all cultural matters; and that way is one that has perturbed thoughtful foreign observers for a long time. In the first place, we may take it for granted that the Jew will disappear as completely from music in Austria as he has already done in Germany, and that the doctrine of the all-over superiority of the Germanic race to any other and the necessity of preserving 'race purity' in music as in everything else, will now be put into still wider practice.

The part that this doctrine has played, is still playing, and will be certain to play in the future, can be realised only by those people in other countries who have followed German literature and German musical journalism during the last few years. The theory that the 'Germanic' race in general, and the German nation in particular, are the source and the repository of all that is valuable in modern civilisation is by no means the product of the last decade or so; on this matter I shall touch one of these days in another article, in which I shall show the curious part played by Wagner and his circle in the flotation and diffusion of this complacent theory. But it is since the Nazis came into power that the theory has passed from the field of learned speculation into that of national practice; and at some of the results of this transition the outside observer can only hold up his hands in blank astonishment. Some German scholars, and several writers who are Germans but not scholars, are hard at work re-writing musical history in terms of this racial prepossession, which the rest of humanity can only regard as fantastic.

Let it not be thought that the world can afford to smile at all this as the aberration of a few theorists, belonging to a nation that has always been a little inclined to let theory go to its head. The consequences of it for the future of music as an international art are vast; it is already manifest that it is going to produce a set of blind prepossessions and prejudices that will radically affect German judgment not only of the music of today and of the future but of the past. Already there are people in Germany turning their virtuous backs on plainsong because it is 'Semitic'. So, in a sense, it is: whatever modifications it underwent in the course of the centuries in the Western Church, it undoubtedly had its origin in oriental habits of thought in general and in synagogue practice in particular. But for many musical thinkers of today the value of plainsong consists precisely in its freedom from the habits of thought that have gradually led to the now too firmly established conventions of modern music—i.e., the Western music of the last two centuries or so.

The entrenchment of our European music in tonality has gradually led to the stifling of melody in the fullest sense of the term, to it becoming a mere upper decoration of two or three basic harmonies, which harmonies exercise so strong a pull upon our invention that melody, in order to accommodate itself to their formal balance of design, has had to confine itself to a lamentably conventional pattern of two or four or eight bar phrases. The Time Spirit has revolted against that convention at last, and the last generation or two has witnessed a convulsive effort to rid music of a tyranny that had become insupportable. The freer rhythmical and accentual structure of pre-harmonic music has become one of the ideals of modern music, with the result that scholars have taken to studying the 'forms' of plain song with a new kind of interest. And now we are being told, in some German quarters, that we should turn our back upon plainsong because it is 'Jewish'!

Musical history, as I have said, is in process of being re-written in Germany. As the doctrine of the prepotency of the 'Germanic' race is sacrosanct, facts have to be brought into a new alignment with it. A quasi-religious importance is being attached to the common chord, as the basis of all real music, because this chord is supposed to be the product of the 'Germanic' race, and a discovery possible only to it. To that race is attributed everything vital in musical history; accordingly one of two things has to be done with non-German composers of the past—either they must be brought, by hook or by crook, into the racial orbit of 'Germanism', or they must be dismissed with a shrug of the shoulders as of far less importance in the history of music than has hitherto been supposed.

A composer, past or present, becomes, for the victims of this delusion, of diminishing significance as it becomes more evident that by no sophistry can he be made to appear 'Germanic.' Above all, the Jew, whether as composer or performer, must be blotted out from the 'Germanic' landscape; and almost everything that is wrong with that landscape, in the opinion of these fanatical theorists, is to be attributed to the malign influence of the Jews. This delusion sometimes takes the strangest forms. For the whole musical world, until quite lately, Joachim, for instance, stood as the noblest type of German musician. But within the last few weeks we have been treated to the spectacle of a German writer calmly attributing Joachim's advice to Clara Schumann not to allow her husband's violin concerto to be published to the fact that truly German music was, and was bound to be, a sealed book to him because of his unfortunate racial origin!

It would be an impertinence on the part of foreigners to advise Germans in the matter of their domestic musical affairs; they have a right to do what they choose in these matters. But a foreigner cannot remain indifferent to the possible effect of the present German attitude towards music on the international future of the art. I have in view now not so much the executive as the creative side of it. On the former side alone, as it seems to us outsiders, Germany will have to pay, and indeed is already paying, a heavy penalty for its ban on all performers who cannot show a hundred per cent Germanic pedigree; already one is becoming painfully conscious that the standard of German performance, from conducting to fiddling, is sinking to one of merely respectable mediocrity. But if the Germans do not mind this, it is no particular concern of the rest of the world, especially as other countries are at present benefiting by the services of performers whose racial or political 'taint' disqualifies them from co-operation in German musical life.

What is really the concern of the whole musical world, however, is the possible and probable result of this narrow racial doctrine upon the future of composition. It has hitherto been the glory of German genius, as Wagner pointed out long ago, to assimilate what was best in the spirit of alien music and to put it to still better uses. Can it make in the future the marvellous progress it has made in the past if it restricts itself to a sort of racial in-breeding, if it rejects the more advanced musical thinking of other races as being at the best 'non-Germanic' and at the worst 'Jewish' or 'Bolshevik'? Time will show; but at the present moment it does not look as if the new 'purity' is on the way to producing results in musical composition anything like as good as the old interfusion.

MUZIKO KAJ ESPERANTO

PER KRITIKISKO ERNEST NEWMAN

February, 1945

NOTHING on earth will induce me to repeat here that flippant little dialogue between a father and his little boy: 'What is Esperanto, Daddy?' 'The universal language, Sonny.' 'Who talks it, Daddy?' 'No-one, Sonny.' For evidently Esperanto is going so strong that even music has now come within its orbit. An eminent pianist, Mr. Frank Merrick, Fratulo kaj Profesoro de la Reĝa Kolegio de Muziko en Londono, has been good enough to send me a 35-page booklet in Esperanto—(*Muzika Terminaro*) compiled by himself and Mr. Montagu C. Butler, Licenciato de la Reĝa Akademio de Muziko en Londono, after konstanta konsulto with a number of other authorities—which contains the Esperanto equivalents of pretty well every word and procedure in use among musicians.

It hurt me, however, to find that the booklet did not mention music critics, and I jumped rather hastily to the conclusion that Esperantists were not aware of the existence of such creatures. Mr. Merrick, however, in response to my wail of anguish, kindly informed me that if Esperantists should ever have occasion to refer to such a person they would call him a muzika kritikisko. These sounds are music in my ears.

I have put in a bit of work at the grammar as set forth in a lucid little *Key to Esperanto* which Mr. Merrick also sends me, and I find that the new language can be fairly easily mastered by anyone, especially if he already has a knowledge of Greek, Latin, French, German, Italian, Spanish and English. That a universal language for musical purposes is a basic need of humanity is proved by the fact that something of the sort sprang spontaneously into being long age: the international use of such words as tempo, forte, piano, crescendo, timbre, reprise and so on is an attempt to agree upon a single word for a constantly recurring thing that will be intelligible to musicians of all countries. Certainly an Englishman, a Bulgarian, a Tibetan and

FROM THE WORLD OF MUSIC

a Laplander could discuss music quite comfortably with the aid of the 'Muzika Terminaro' of Mr. Merrick and Mr. Butler. 'Sonata formo', for instance, is shown to consist of (a) an Anonca Sekcio with a Unua (Ĉefa) Subjekto and a Dua(Flanka) Subjekto, (b) an Ellabora Sekcio (ofte kun nova materialo), and (c) a Resuma Sekcio; while a Simfonio is tersely but lucidly defined as a verko sonateca por orkestro.

The difficulties would begin, I imagine, when the above-mentioned Esperantists who had got that far wanted to extend their knowledge of sonata formo by studying Hugo Riemann, Schenker, Hadow, d'Indy and a few others, in which case they would have to learn German, English, French and one or two other ancient European languages.

I imagine that Esperanto would prove very useful in the teaching of music to a class of students drawn from all nations, and, again, when a foreigner, ignorant of our local speech, was conducting an English orchestra—presupposing that our orchestral players had taken the trouble to learn the universal tongue. But in that case they would lose all the good clean fun they get at present out of hearing these foreigners striving to communicate their wishes in English. Some years ago a foreign opera conductor got very angry with the Covent Garden orchestra for chattering so much at rehearsal. He wanted to tell them plainly that while he didn't mind a reasonable amount of this sort of thing there were limits to what he was prepared to put up with. I gather, after a brief study of the *Key to Esperanto*, that if he and the players had all been Esperantists he would have admonished them in this fashion: 'Ne parolu! Mi pov toleri ĝi tiam kaj nun sed ciam mia Di neniam.' (Esperanto stylists who read this may shudder at my ignorance of the finer points of the language; but I am only a learner as yet.)

What the conductor actually said was something that will always be inscribed in letters of gold on tablets of ivory in the annals of Covent Garden: "Don't spoke! I can stand it then and now but always my God never!" I greatly prefer it in this form, and so, I am sure, would the orchestral players: little things of that kind mean a great deal in their drab lives.